A WORLD GUIDE TO WHISK(E)Y DISTILLERIES

Compiled for the American Distilling Institute
**by Eric Abram Zandona
and Nancy Fraley**
with contributions by
Julia Nourney and Bill Owens

Published by

WHITE MULE PRESS

© **WHITE MULE PRESS**
AMERICAN DISTILLING INSTITUTE
2013
ALL RIGHTS RESERVED.
ISBN 978-0-9836389-4-0
P.O. BOX 577
HAYWARD, CA 94541

VISIT THE AMERICAN DISTILLING INSTITUTE WEBSITE AT
WWW.DISTILLING.COM

Contents

vi	Preface
xii	Introduction
3	Africa
7	Asia
19	Australia | New Zealand
25	Europe
49	England | Ireland | Wales
55	Scotland
75	Canada
81	USA Whiskey Distilleries
87	USA Craft Distilleries
125	Latin America
133	Appendices

Distilleries operated by major conglomerates
Maps

Preface

The *World Guide to Whisk(e)y[1] Distilleries* is an attempt to collect all of the world's whisk(e)y distilleries into one volume. While there are many informative and beautiful books on whisky, ours is quite different. It does not try to list or rate every whisky brand made for two reasons: One, there are a number of books and websites that already do this; and two, these books tend to obscure the fact that there are far fewer whisky distilleries than whisky brands. If one were to look at the whisky selection available at an average US supermarket or liquor store, it would be easy to assume that there are a lot of different companies producing a wide variety of whisky. The truth, however, is that most of the brands on the shelves are produced at only a handful of distilleries. It is a common practice for large spirit companies to blend the whiskies produced at a few of their distilleries into several different bottlings; the only difference being the ratio or ages of the whiskies going into the blend. Some distilleries also sell their whisky to independent bottlers who will blend and bottle the spirits under their own label. Consequently, it should not come as a shock to the reader if they do not find their favorite blended whisky in this book. At the same time, I hope that this book can help demystify the whisky selection at the local store or bar so that you, the reader, can know exactly where the whisky you see on the shelves comes from and who makes it.

When Bill Owens first brought up the idea of working on a book of all the whisky distilleries in the world, I was intrigued and it seemed like a great opportunity to add to my knowledge of the whisky world. As a historian and enthusiastic whisky drinker, I thought I knew a fair amount about it but this project has contributed a great deal to my knowledge of current trends in global whisky production. As can be expected, the project took longer to complete than I originally expected and it revealed people and places around the world that I never would have associated with whisky production.

One of the first tasks of researching and writing this book was to determine which producers to include and which to leave out. This might sound odd considering the goal of the book but I and the other contributors decided that this book would strive to include all the active commercial producers of whisky. However, accomplishing this goal was complicated by a few factors. First, there is no single global definition for whisky. Second, each country sets its own standards and legal framework for how commercial distilleries are licensed. Third, what to consider an active producer in an industry that is rapidly growing.

---

[1] A quick note about spelling. As many may know or notice, there are two common spellings for the name of the aged grain spirit we call whiskey or whisky. While there are a number of historical and contemporary exceptions to the rule, the United States and Ireland usually spell whiskey with an e and while the rest of the world spells whisky without an e. While spelling whisk(e)y with the parentheses is technically correct when referring to aged grain spirits that use both names it is also visually cumbersome. Therefore in an attempt at simplify these introductory remarks, the spelling without an e will be used when referring to whisky in general or in the instances when both spellings are appropriate.

In the light of these complications, three choices were made in an attempt to create the most comprehensive guide of the world's whisky distilleries. First, I have decided to stay out of any debate about the definition of whisky and adopted the accepted (often the legal) definition of whisky for whatever country the distillery resides in. This means that whisky made in the European Union is an all grain spirit aged for at least three years in wood barrels. Whereas, in the United States the basic definition of whiskey requires, among other things, that the spirit be stored in oak barrels, but it does not specify for how long.

The second decision was to only include commercial distilleries, which are distinguished in most countries by the requirement to hold a license or permit to operate. The one major exception to this are the Austrian, German and Swiss distilleries. Germany has two different licenses for distillers. The first is similar to licenses in Scotland and has two major requirements: the distillery must hold a bond to cover the excise tax for the amount of alcohol produced; and, the distillery must install a number of physical barriers that prevent any alcohol from being diverted and uncounted for tax purposes. In return, the distillery is allowed to produce as much alcohol as they want, whenever they want. The second type of license allows a person to operate a still and produce up to 300 liters of pure alcohol per year for their business. These distillers can also contract with farmers, who have a special permit, to produce up to 50 liters of spirits which does not count toward their personal businesses 300 liter limit. Currently there are about 33,000 of these small-distiller licenses in Germany though not all of them are being used and most are producing unaged spirits that are only sold locally. Austria and Switzerland have similar licenses for small distillers so I and the other contributors to this book decided to exclude these small unbonded distilleries to maintain the book's focus on distilleries engaged in the broader commercial whisky markets within their own country or internationally.

The final decision was, at what point to stop including new distilleries. Almost every week a new company forms somewhere around the world with the plans of operating a distillery and producing whisky. I decided to end my research phase after about six months of full-time searching and outreach. And while I have attempted to be as comprehensive as possible, the nature of the subject reinforces the fact that what follows is only a snapshot in time of the whisky distilleries that are currently active. In some instances I have included non-productive distilleries that at the time of my research were likely to begin producing whisky within the next year. Here I would like to say to any whisky distillery that was missed, please feel free to contact the American Distilling Institute and we would be happy to talk to you about inclusion in future editions of this book.

One question that is bound to be raised is, "Why produce this as a book and not a website?" The simple answer is that the internet can and often does give a false impression that the information it contains is complete and accurate. As a book, this compilation holds a few of advantages. First, its organization and construction allows for easy navigation. Second, it allows the reader, at a glance, to compare and contrast distilleries within a region and with other regions. Third, as a book there is no implicit claim of perpetual accuracy. At the same time this book would not have been possible, or at the very least, difficult and expensive to produce without the internet. During the course of my research I came across a number of very helpful websites and blogs that focus on Scotch or Bourbon and even a couple that take a global perspective. But like many things that exist on the web, the information contained was sometimes incorrect and very often the sites had no date of publication or when a particular page was last updated. Because of this, much of the information in this book came directly from the companies themselves. I am grateful to all the distillers who took the time to talk to me about their whisky. However when direct contact with the company was not possible, at least two other sources were utilized to verify individual entries.

Acknowlegements

I would like to acknowledge and thank my fellow contributors, Nancy Fraley, Julia Nourney, and Bill Owens. Without their help it would have been very difficult to fulfill the goal of the book and it would not have been nearly as thorough. In particular, Julia was instrumental in helping me understand whiskey production and the licensing system in the German speaking counties, as well as keeping me focused on their bonded distilleries. I would also like to thank Dave Broom for providing helpful notes and insight about whiskey production in Japan. Gail Sands helped me proof the manuscript and has done a wonderful job of designing the layout of the book. Thank you to Bill for trusting me to carry this project through to completion. Finally, I would like to thank my wife who has been a great source of support and encouragement throughout this entire process.

Introduction

This book bears witness to two contrary global trends in the business of whisky production. In the last couple of decades, whisky production has consolidated under the control of ten major companies and seen the birth of hundreds of new companies. Through mergers and acquisitions, companies like Diageo and Pernod Ricard dominate the global production of Scotch and Irish whisky. In the United States, Beam Global, Brown-Forman, and Sazerac produce and own the majority of the established American whiskey brands, as well as many of the Canadian whisky distilleries. These global companies operate on an impressively massive scale that measures their daily production in units of 100,000 liters, making the ubiquity of their products possible.

During this same period, there has been a growing number of small independent whisky distilleries opening in the United States, Australia, and Switzerland. The United States has seen the majority of this growth, and even though this book contains almost 250 distilleries producing whisky in the US, this is less than one tenth of the all the distilleries that operated before National Prohibition in 1920. Due to a variety of factors, many of these new distilleries are attempting to create space for themselves in the marketplace by highlighting their pre-prohibition roots, emphasizing the use of locally grown or organic grains and attempting to create new regional styles of whisky. In Switzerland, the whisky boom began in earnest after a ban on the production of whisky was repealed in 1999. The ban, which lasted for about a century, was a wartime measure meant to ensure that starches and grains were used for food production rather than spirits. Since the ban was lifted almost two-dozen Swiss distilleries have begun producting whisky. The proliferation of Swiss and Australian whisky distilleries indicates a growing demand for whisky generally, and for local craft spirits internationally.

Asia was a surprising region to research. Japan is well known for their whiskies that tend to be modeled after un-peated Scotch and China and India are important, fast growing consumers and producers in the whisky world. Since China's entry into the World Trade Organization in 2001, the demand for Scotch has increased so much that Diageo announced in July 2012 a £1 billion investment over the next five years to increase their production. Despite this huge demand, China only has one whisky distillery on the island of Taiwan. At the same time, India, which is not well known internationally for its alcohol production, is producing, and apparently selling, very large quantities of locally made spirits, including whisky. Most of the Indian whisky distilleries are making very large quantities of what they call extra neutral alcohol and blending it with imported Scotch, while some of these distilleries are producing their own Indian Malt Whisky.

This worldwide love of whisky is due, in part, because it is simultaneously simple and complex. Whisky is made from three simple ingredients: grain, water, and yeast. Yet the wide variety of grains used, the shape of the still, the choices made during distillation, the multiple barrel types to age the whisky, the length of maturation and even the environmental variations where the whisky is stored, creates hundreds and hundreds of variables that create layers of complexity that give each whisky its own unique character. This dual nature of whisky's simplicity and complexity contributes to its enduring popularity and its ability to inspire.

Distilleries like Bushmills in Ireland and Strathisla in Scotland have been operating since the late eighteenth century; and Jack Daniel's, the United States' longest operating distillery, has been open since 1866. These companies and many others tap into whisky's ability to evoke feelings of tradition and craftsmanship. They also reinforce the idea that whisky production is a stable business that can withstand the test to time. Yet like other businesses, whisky producers are vulnerable to changes in consumer tastes, government regulations, and global business trends. While there is no doubt that some of the distilleries in this book will not survive to the next edition, it is also true that many more will open to take their place. Ultimately, I hope that you, the reader, will enjoy perusing this book and learn something from it; whether it is about a new whisky distillery in your own backyard or one on the other side of the world.

Cheers,
Eric Zandona
July 2012

SOURCES

Carrell, Severin. "Diageo to exploit global demand for whisky with £1bn investment." *The Guardian*, June 6, 2012. Accessed July 20, 2012. www.guardian.co.uk/business/2012/jun/06/diageo-exploit-global-demand-whisky.

Fletcher, Clementine. "Remy Cointreau Full-Year Profit Gains On Asian Demand." *Bloomberg*, June 12, 2012. Accessed July 21, 2012. www.bloomberg.com/news/2012-06-12/remy-cointreau-full-year-profit-gains-on-asian-demand.html.

Lu, Liu. "Seeking a measure of success." *China Daily*, November 10 2011. Accessed July 21, 2012. www.chinadaily.com.cn/bizchina/2011-11/10/content_14069690.htm

Pre-Pro. "The pre-Prohibition Distillery Database." Accessed July 20, 2012. www.pre-pro.com/midacore/distillery_index.php

Africa

Drayman's Distillery | South Africa

Drayman's Distillery Drayman's offers a single malt whisky, matured in former 4th or 5th fill red wine barrels made from American oak, which have been seasoned with ale made at the distillery's brewery. [page 5]

ANGOLA

INDUSTRIAS ALIMENTARES REUNIDAS
Av Paulo Dias Novais,
Bairro da Luz - Lobito
Angola
Tel: +24472210104
They produce Black Horse and John Johnston Whiskies.

KENYA

AFRICAN SPIRITS LTD
Physical Address:
ShimoLa Tewa Rd.
Off Mombasa Rd.
Nairobi
Kenya
Postal Address:
P.O. BOX 61479–00200
Nairobi
Kenya
Tel: +254 722 509834
Email: info@africaspirits.co.ke
www.africaspirits.co.ke
They produce Furaha Blended Whisky and bottle Two Keys Scotch Whisky.

ERDEMANN PROPERTY EPZ LTD
PO Box 42541-001000
Nairobi
Kenya
Tel: +254 20 6763981
Email: erdemann@wananchi.com
They produce Tiger Whisky.

UNITED DISTILLERS AND VINTERS LTD
Kampala Rd.
Indstrial Area
Nairobi
Kenya
Tel: +254 20 5531422
Email: info@eabl.com
www.eabl.com/
A subsidiary of both East African Brewers Ltd and Diageo, they produce Bond 7 Blended Whisky.

SOUTH AFRICA

DRAYMAN'S DISTILLERY
Physical Address:
222 Dykor Rd.
Silverton Pretoria 0127
South Africa
Postal Address:
PO Box 1648
Silverton Pretoria 0127
South Africa
Tel: +27 (0) 12 804 8800
Email: info@draymans.co.za
www.draymans.com
Drayman's offers a single malt whisky, matured in former 4th or 5th fill red wine barrels made from American oak, which have been seasoned with ale made at the distillery's brewery.

JAMES SEDGWICK DISTILLERY
Physical Address:
Aan-de-Wagenweg
Stellenbosch 7600
South Africa
Postal Address:
PO Box 184
Stellenbosch 7599
South Africa
Tel: +27(0)21 - 809 7000
Email: info@distell.co.za
www.distell.co.za
James Sedgwick produces Bain's Cape Mountain Whisky, South Africa's first single grain whisky. They also produce three brands that are blends of South African and Scottish whiskies. They are Knights, Harrier, and Three Ships Whisky.

ZIMBABWE

AFRICAN DISTILLERS
Stapleford
Harare
Zimbabwe
Tel: +263 4 2915301
Email: sales@afdis.co.zw
www.africandistillers.com/
They produce a variety of spirits including Gold Blend Whisky.

HAKUSHU | JAPAN

HAKUSHU DISTILLERY, located in the foothills of the Southern Japanese Alps and owned by Suntory, produces whisky for a variety of Suntory's blends and for single malt bottlings. The range of Hakushu single malt expressions includes a 12, 18, and 25 year old expressions.
[page 13]

Asia

Amrut | India

Amrut Distilleries currently produces five malt expressions: Amrut Indian Single Malt Whisky bottled at 46% abv and Cask Strength; Amrut Peated Indian Single Malt Whisky bottled at 46% abv and Cask Strength; and Amrut Fusion Single Malt Whisky, a blend of Indian and Scotch Malt Whisky. [page 9]

BHUTAN

GAYLEGPHUG DISTILLERY
Army Welfare Project
Gaylegphug Distillery Gaylegphug
HO Post Box No. 92
Dewang Apartment
Pelkhil House, 5th Floor
Phuntsholing
Bhutan
Produces Bhutan Mist Pure Malt Whisky and Coronation Silver Jubilee Whisky.

INDIA

AMRUT DISTILLERIES, LTD.
#41/1 72nd Cross
Rajajinagar 6th Block
Bangalore 560010
India
Tel: +91 80 23100402, 308, 379, 389
Email: Built into their website
www.amrutwhisky.co.uk
Amrut distillery currently produces five malt expressions: Amrut Indian Single Malt Whisky bottled at 46% abv and Cask Strength; Amrut Peated Indian Single Malt Whisky bottled at 46% abv and Cask Strength; and Amrut Fusion Single Malt Whisky, a blend of Indian and Scotch Malt Whisky.

CHANDIGARH DISTILLERS & BOTTLERS LTD
Banur, District
Patiala Punjab
Tel: +91 1762-251427, 251727, 507064, 507065, 506067
Email: rajeev@cdblindia.com
www.cdblindia.com
They produce Big Boss and After 7 Whisky as well as Grain, Molasses, and Industrial Alcohol for other companies.

EMPEE DISTILLERIES, LTD.
Mevaloorkuppam
Sriperumbudur Taluk
Kancheepuram Dist.
Chennai 600002
India
Tel: +91 27156235, 27156239/360/728
Email: info@empeegroup.co.in
www.empeegroup.co.in/empee_distilleries.htm
They operate a few distilleries spread out over Southern India and produce a couple different brands of malt whisky. They include Empee's Premium Gold Whisky and Power Whisky. They are in the process of expanding their operation to begin offering a value whisky brand too.

JAGATJIT
4th Floor, Bhandari House
91 Nehru Place
New Delhi
India
www.jagatjit.com
Jagatjit produces a line of malt whisky under the Aristocrat Malt Whiskey brand. They also produce two economy brands Binnies Whisky and Shatranj Blended Whisky

KHEMANI DISTILLERIES PVT LTD
Ringanwada, Kachigam Rd.
Daman U.T. 396210
India
Tel: +91 260 224 2672
Email: info@khemanigroup.com
www.khemanigroup.com
They produce five different bottlings of blended Indian Malt, including Royal's Special and Hex Fine Whisky.

KHODAY INDIA LTD
"Brewery House," 7th Mile,
Kanakapura Rd.
Bangalore 560062
India
Tel: +91 80 22956570-5
Email: Built into their website
www.khodayindia.com
Khoday produces Peter Scot Whisky.

MOHAN MEAKIN
Solan Distillery and Brewery
Shimla Hills, H.P. 173214 Himachal Pradesh
India
Tel: +91 1792 230450
www.mohanmeakin.com
Products include Black Knight Blended Whisky, Diplomat Deluxe Blended Whisky, and Royal Victoria Blended Whisky.

NV GROUP
10th Floor, Vandana Building
11, Tolstoy Marg, Connaught Place
New Delhi 110001
India
Tel: +91 011 43107000
Email: Built into their website
www.nvgroup.co.in
They operate a number of distilleries across India that primarily produce Extra Neutral Alcohol. Their Party Special Platinum Whisky is a blend of their Indian grain and malt spirits with imported Scotch Whisky.

YAMAZAKI | JAPAN

YAMAZAKI is currently owned by Suntory. Yamazaki is the oldest whisky distillery in Japan and is known for its Single Malt Whiskies which are aged 10, 12, 18, 25, 35 and 50 years. They also produce Hibiki blended whiskies. Some of their whiskies are finished in Japanese oak
[page 15]

PREMIER DISTILLERIES PVT LTD
R.S.No.62/8, Madukarai Rd.
Mangalam Village, Villianur Commune,
Puducherry 605110
India
Tel: +91 0413 - 2221432, 2221433
Email: info@premierdistilleries.com
www.premierdistilleries.com
They produce Delight Fine Whisky and Malbar Malt Whisky.

RADICO KHAITAN
Plot J-I, Block B-1
Mohan Co-operative Industrial Area
Mathura Rd.
New Delhi
India
Tel: +91 11 40975400/5500
Email: Built into their website
www.radicokhaitan.com
Radico Khaitan produces a range of blended whiskies, including 8PM, 8PM Royale Whiskey, Whythall Whisky, and After Dark Fine Grain Whisky.

RAVIKUMAR DISTILLERIES LIMITED
No. 17, Kamaraj Salai,
Puducherry 605011
India
Tel: +91 413 2343278 / 2331032
Email: sales@ravikumardistilleries.com
www.ravikumardistilleries.com
They produce a wide variety of spirits including: Capricorn Super Premium Whisky, which is a blend of vatted Scotch malt and Indian spirits; 2 Barrels Blended Whisky, which is a blend of Scotch and Indian grain spirits; Duplex Fine Whisky; Konarak Malt Whisky, which is a blend of matured malt spirits and Indian fine spirits; Chevalier Whisky, which is a blend of matured Indian malt and extra neutral alcohol.

SAINOV SPIRITS PVT LTD
409, 4th Floor, Elegance Tower 8
Jasola District Center
New Delhi 110076,
India
Tel: +91 11 40691351
Email: contact@sainov.com
www.sainov.com
They bottle Old McDonald Scotch Whisky and produce Ninja Whisky which is a blended whisky from Indian Malt and Neutral Grain Spirits and a second Ginger flavored whisky.

SOM DISTILLERIES & BREWERIES PVT. LTD
23, Zone-II Maharana Paratap Nagar
Bhopal
Madhya Pradesh
India
Tel: + 91 755 4271271
Email: Built into website
www.tradeindia.com/Seller-2786390-SOM-Distilleries-Breweries-Pvt-Ltd-/
They produce four different brands of whisky: 21st Century, Gypsy Fine, He Man XXX, and Super Master Whisky.

TILAKNAGAR INDUSTRIES LTD
3rd Floor, Industrial Assurance Building
Churchgate
Mumbai 400020
India
Tel: +91 22 2283 1718/16
Email: tiliquor@tilind.com
www.tilind.com/product_whisky.html
They produce 12 different brands of blended whisky. Some are blends of Indian and Scotch whisky while others are blends of Indian Malt and Neutral Grain Spirits.

UNITED SPIRITS LTD
UB Tower
24 Vittal Mallya Rd.
Bangalore 560001
India
Tel: +91-80-39856500
Email: contactus@ubmail.com
www.unitedspirits.in/usl-whisky.aspx
United Spirits produces a wide range of spirits and operates 21 distilleries throughout India, some of which produce Indian Malt Whisky. They market their Indian Malt in 6 brands: Antiquity, No. 1 McDowells's, Royal Challenge, Director's Special and Signature, which are blends of Indian Malt and Scotch Whisky at varying price points; Bagpiper Deluxe Whisky is a blended Indian Malt Whisky from their various distilleries.

YOICHI | JAPAN

YOICHI The second of Nikka's distilleries, Yoichi is known for producing a richer, peatier malt than the Sendai distillery. Yoichi produces a 10 year old single cask malt, and a Yoichi Single Malt of unspecified age, as well as a 10, 12, 15, and 20 year old. [see Nikka page 13]

JAPAN

CHICHIBU DISTILLERY
Venture Whisky
49 Midorigaoka
Chichibu-shi
Saitama
Japan
Tel: +81 494 62 4601
Email: tokyo@one-drinks.com
www.one-drinks.com/chichibu.php

This new distillery was opened in Spring 2008 by Ichiro Akuto, the grandson of the founder of the now defunct Hanyu distillery. Products include Ichiro's Malt Chichibu "Newborn Series:" New Hogshead, and Bourbon Barrel which were only aged for a few months before bottling. They also offer two aged whiskies: The First and The Peated.

FUJI-GOTEMBA
970 Shibanuta
Gotemba Shizuoka 412-0003,
Japan
Tel: +81 550 89 3131
Email: Built into their website
www.kirin.co.jp/english

The Fuji-Gotemba distillery, owned by Kirin (formerly Kirin-Seagrams), is known for producing a number of light style whiskies, including the Fuji-Gotemba 18-Year Old, and the Fuji-Gotemba Single Grain 15-Year Old.

HAKUSHU
2913-1 Torihara, Hakushu-cho
Hokuto-shi, Yamanashi
Japan
Tel: +81 551 35 2211
www.suntory.com/whisky/en/distilleries/hakushu.html

Currently owned by Suntory, Hakushu is a single malt distillery. It produces a number of different styles of distillate most of which are used in blends, though they are also starting to produce Single malt bottlings.

HANYU
Tel: +81 0 3 5418 4611
Email: tokyo@one-drinks.com
www.one-drinks.com/hanyu.php

The grandson of the founder of this now defunct distillery rescued 400 casks of malt whisky, and is releasing it under the "Ichiro's Malt label as a Card Series. Bottled from individual casks, this series varies both in age and ABV.

KARUIZAWA
Maseguchi 1795-2, Oaza
Miyotamachi, Kitasakugun, Nagano
Email: tokyo@one-drinks.com
www.one-drinks.com/karuizawa.php

This small distillery used only Golden Promise barley sourced from the UK in its malts, and then ages them in American Oak and Sherry butts. Since its closure the remaining stock is distributed by Number One Drinks Company. Expressions include the Karuizawa Vintage Single Cask 1988 and the Karuizawa Vintage Single Cask 1992.

MARS DISTILLERY
4752-31 Miyata-mura
Kamiinagun
Nagano Prefecture 399-4301
Japan
Tel: +81 0265 85 4633

Mars started production in 2011 after 17 years of silence. Some old stock is currently being sold as cask and vintage bottlings.

NIKKA WHISKY DISTILLING CO LTD
5-4-31, Minami-Aoyama, Minato-ku,
Tokyo 107-8616,
Japan
Tel: +81 3 3498 0331
Email: Built into their website
www.nikka.com/eng

They operate the Yoichi and Miyagikyo distilleries and produce three brands of single malt whisky and ten blended whisky brands. The Yoichi distillery uses a coal fired still which might contribute to the rich oily notes in the single malt.

WHITE OAK WHISKY DISTILLERY (EIGASHIMA SHUZO)
919 Nishijima
Ookubo-cho
Akashi-shi 674-0065
Japan
Tel: +81 078 946 1001
Email: info@ei-sake.jp
www.ei-sake.jp

This seaside plant produces both Shochu and Akashi Single Malt Whisky.

MIYAGIKYO | JAPAN

MIYAGIKYO DISTILLERY. One of two distilleries owned by Nikka. Miyagikyo produces a line of lighter, fragrant whiskies that includes three single malts, aged 10, 12, and 15 years, and a single cask whisky. [see Nikka page 13]

YAMAZAKI
5-2-1 Yamazaki
Shimamoto-cho,
Mishima-gun
Osaka
Japan
Tel: +81 75 962 1423
www.suntory.com/whisky/en/distilleries/yamazaki.html

Currently owned by Suntory. Yamazaki is the oldest whisky distillery in Japan and is known for its Single Malt Whiskies which are aged 10, 12, 18, 25, 35 and 50 years. They also produce Hibiki blended whiskies. Some of their whiskies are finished in Japanese oak.

LAOS

INTER SPIRITS (LAO) CO LTD
NongdouangNeua
Vientiane Cap
Laos
Tel: +856 21 26 4315
Email: interspirits@yahoo.com

Their Champa Whisky is a blend of vatted Scotch Malt Whisky with locally produced grain spirits.

TIGER WHISKY FACTORY
086 07 Xaimoungkhoun
Vientiane Cap
Laos
Tel: +856-21 6407 08

They produce Super Tiger Blended Whisky.

MYANMAR

MYANMAR BREWERY AND DISTILLERY
No. 45, No. 3 Trunk Rd.
Pyinmabin Industrial Complex
Mingaladon Township, Yangon
Myanmar
Tel: +95 1-636258

Myanmar Brewery and Distillery is the producer of Thistle Mandalay Malt Whisky.

MYANMAR WINERY & DISTILLERY CO. LTD
No. R-18, S-19, Sittaung St.
Pyinnyawaddy Ave.
Yankin Township, Yangon
Myanmar
Tel: +95 1 557441
www.rubtumweb.com/work/ibtc/mwdc.html#

They produce Grand Royal Special Reserve Whisky and Eagle Whisky.

PEACE MYANMAR GROUP CO. LTD.
No. 42/63 (Kha) Sethmu 1st St.
Ward 1, Shwepyitha Industrial Zone
Shwepyitha Township, Yangon
Myanmar
Tel: +95 0 1 610 049
Email: Built into their website
www.pmgmyanmar.com

Peace Myanmar Group makes Myanmar Whisky and Premier Whisky.

NEPAL

HIGHLAND DISTILLERY PVT. LTD.
P.O. Box 7207 Plaza Tripureshwor
Kathmandu
Nepal
Tel: +97714265758
Email: hdpl@info.com.np

They produce Challenger Blended Whisky and Virgin Whisky.

NEPAL DISTILLERIES PVT LTD
Balaju
Kathmandu
Nepal
Tel: +97 7 1 350725
Email: info@nepaldistilleries.com

Founded in 1960, they produce John Bull Blended Whisky and Old Reserve Whisky.

SHREE DISTILLERY
13860, Ktm Naxal
Kathmandu
Nepal
Tel: +97 4416330
Email: shreeo@mos.com.np

They make Mt. Everest Whisky which is a combination of imported malt spirit and Nepalese Extra Neutral Alcohol.

SUMY DISTILLERY PVT. LTD.
P.O. Box 8975, EPC 5407
Shangrila Complex, Maharajgunj
Chakrapath, Kathmandu
Nepal
Email: sumy@mos.com.np
www.sumy.com.np
Tel: +977-1-4720818

Products include Gill Marry Blended Whisky.

King Car Distillery | Taiwan

King Car Yuan-Shan Taiwan's only whisky distillery first bottled their Kavalan Single Malt in 2008. They currently offer a wide selection of whiskies that have been aged or finished in bourbon, port, sherry, and wine barrels. [page 17]

PAKISTAN

MURREE
National Park Rd.
P.O. Box No. 13
Rawalpindi, Pakistan
Tel: +92 051 5567041 7
Email: admin@murreebrewery.com, murbr@cyber.net.pk, murreebrewery@cybernet.pk
www.murreebrewery.com

This brewery is also Pakistan's only distillery producing single malts. They produce a 3, 8, 12, and 21-year old malt whisky. Their Vintage whisky is a blend of Pakistani malt and Scotch whisky. The distillery uses oak casks sourced from Australia, Spain and North America.

PHILIPPINES

CONSOLIDATED DISTILLERS OF THE FAR EAST, INC
2nd Floor Alliance Global Bldg.
188 Eastwood Ave
Quezon City 1110
Philippines
Tel: +63 2 439-7500

They produce two blended whiskies, APS Whisky and Collector's Whisky.

DESTILERIA LIMTUACO
1830 E. Delos Santos Ave. Quezon City Metro
Manila, 1106
Philippines
Tel: +63 632 3617491
Email: limtuaco@limtuacodistillery.com
www.limtuaco.com/

Established in 1852 they produce a wide variety of spirits including two whiskies. White Castle 5-Year Old Whisky is a distilled malt spirits and aged in Oak. White Castle Calibre 69 Whisky is a blend of their White Castle 5 and imported malt spirits which is then aged in oak.

SRI LANKA

PERICEYL PVT LTD.
81 A 1/1 Temple Rd.
Nawala
Sri Lanka.
Tel: +94 11 5762249/2808565
Email: periceylgm@bellmail.lk
www.dcslgroup.com/periceyl.aspx

They manufacture a variety of distilled spirits including House of Tilbury Whisky and Tillsider Whisky.

TAIWAN

KING CAR YUAN-SHAN WHISKY DISTILLERY
326, Sec. 2, Yuan-Shan Rd.
Yuan-Shan Township, Yilan Count 264
Taiwan
Tel: +886 3 9229000, ex. # 1104
Email: Built into their website
www.kavalanwhisky.com

Taiwan's only whisky distillery first bottled their Kavalan Single Malt in 2008. They currently offer a wide selection of whiskies that have been aged or finished in bourbon, port, sherry, and wine barrels.

THAILAND

RED BULL DISTILLERY
Office:
15 Moo 14
Vibhavadi Rangsit Rd.
Chomphon Sub-District
Chatuchak District
Bangkok 10900
Thailand
Tel: +66 02 278 4321
Distillery:
8 Moo 5
Setthakit 1 Rd.
Tambon Nadee Amphoe
Muang District,
Samut Sakhon 74000
Thailand
Tel: +66 034 830 213-6
www.thaibev.com/en08/home.aspx

They produce Crown 99 and Blend 285 whiskies by blending aged Scotch whisky with their own neutral grain spirits and purified water, then bottled at 35% abv.

Bakery Hill | Austrlia

Bakery Hill distillery currently offers five single malt and single cask whiskies, which include two Peated and two Classic malts (both expressions are also available in cask strength), and a Double Wood version aged in former bourbon and French oak. [page 21]

AUSTRALIA | NEW ZEALAND

Lark | Australia

Lark They produce 5 year old Lark Single Malt Whiskey, Lark Pure Malt Spirit, and Slainte, a single malt whisky liqueur with herbs and spices. [page 21]

AUSTRALIA

BAKERY HILL DISTILLERY
28 Ventnor St.
North Balwyn, Victoria 3104
Australia
Tel: + 61 3 9857 7070
Email: david@bakeryhilldistillery.com.au
www.bakeryhilldistillery.com.au

Bakery Hill distillery currently offers five single malt and single cask whiskies, which include two Peated and two Classic malts (both expressions are also available in cask strength), and a Double Wood version aged in former bourbon and French oak.

BELGROVE DISTILLERY
3121 Midland Hwy.
Kempton, Tasmania 7030
Australia
Email: Built into their website
www.belgrovedistillery.com.au

Opened in 2010 by Peter Bignell, the farm distillery is growing its own rye and producing a 100% rye spirit in a handmade copper still that is direct fired by biodiesel. Bignell is maturing some of the whisky in oak which will sold as Belgrove Rye Whisky.

COROWA WHISKY & CHOCOLATE PYT LTD.
20-24 Steel St.
Corowa, New South Whales 2646
Australia
Tel: +61 0260 331 311
Email: dean@corowawhiskyandchocolate.com.au
www.corowawhisky.com

They are planning to manufacture and mature an organic single malt whisky that is aged at least 7 years before being bottled.

GREAT SOUTHERN DISTILLING COMPANY
1st Floor, Empire Building
146-152 Stirling Terrace
Albany, Western Australia 6330
Australia
Tel: +61 08 9842 2046
Email: info@distillery.com.au
www.distillery.com.au

Great Southern Distilling Company, the first legal distillery in Western Australia, releases only single barrel expressions of their malt whisky, known as "Limeburners Western Australian Single Malt Whisky."

HELLYERS ROAD
153 Old Surrey Rd. (PO Box 1415)
Burnie, Tasmania 7320
Australia
Tel: + 61 03 6433 0439
Email: sales@hellyersroaddistillery.com.au
www.hellyersroaddistillery.com.au

This Tasmanian distillery is Australia's largest, complete with computer controlled, automated stills. They produce six variations of their single malt whisky: Original, 10-year old, Peated, Slightly Peated, Pinot Noir Finish and Southern Fire. They also produce three whisky cream liqueurs with their single malt. They come in Original, Coffee and Hazelnut.

HOOCHERY DISTILLERY
300 Weaber Plain Rd.
Kununurra, Western Australia 6743
Australia
Tel: + 61 08 9168 2467
Email: hoochery@hoochery.com.au
www.hoochery.com.au

The oldest continuously operating distillery in Western Australia produces Raymond B. Whisky, made of 100% corn mash.

LARK DISTILLERY
14 Davey St.
Hobart, Tasmania 7000
Australia
Tel: + 61 3 6231 9088
Email: info@larkdistillery.com.au
www.larkdistillery.com.au

They produce 5-year old Lark Single Malt Whiskey, Lark Pure Malt Spirit, and Slainte, a single malt whisky liqueur with herbs and spices.

MACKEY'S DISTILERY
116 New Town Rd.
New Town, Tasmania 7008
Australia
Tel: +61 362782506
www.mackeysdistillery.com.au

Mackey is using a 300 liter still to triple distill 100% unpeated malted barley and then aging the whisky in 100 liter port barrels.

NANT DISTILLERY
Nant Estate
Nant Lane
PO Box 4
Bothwell, Tasmania 7030
Australia
Tel: +61 03 6259 5790
Email: info@nantdistillery.com.au
www.nantdistillery.com.au
Founded in 2005 Nant distillery debuted with its first release, The Nant Vatted Malt, in November 2008. It is currently producing Tasmanian Single Malt Whisky from 100% Tasmanian grown malted barley.

OLD HOBART DISTILLERY
Tasmania, Australia
Email: info@oldhobartdistillery.com
oldhobartdistillery.com
Opened in 2005, they produce "The Singular Overeem Single Malt Whisky" matured in Port or Sherry casks and bottled either at 43% abv or cask strength.

SMALL CONCERN DISTILLERY
P.O Box 14
Ulverstone, Tasmania 7315
Australia
Tel: +61 03 6429 1208
Email: davidmaclennan@bigpond.com
www.tasmanianwhisky.com.au
Products include the triple distilled Cradle Mountain Single Malt Whisky and Cradle Mountain Double Malt, a blend of Cradle Mountain Single Malt and Springbank Single Malt from Campbelltown, Scotland.

SOUTHERN COAST DISTILLERS
2/154 Fredrick St.
Welland, Southern Australia 5007
Australia
Email: Built into their website
southerncoastdistillers.com.au
They produce malt whisky that is matured in refurbished Port and Sherry casks. The whisky is labeled by batch number and bottled at 46% abv.

TASMANIA DISTILLERY
1/14 Lamb Place,
Cambridge, Tasmania 7170
Australia
Tel: +61 03 6248 5399
Email: Built into their website
www.tasmaniadistillery.com
Products include the Sullivan's Cove Single Barrel Cask Strength and Sullivan's Cove Single Barrel Cask Strength Port Finish. They also produced a single malt whisky for Trapper's Hut.

TIMBOON RAILWAY SHED DISTILLERY
The Railway Yard, Bailey St.,
Timboon, Victoria 3268
Australia
Tel: +61 03 5598 3555
Email: info@timboondistillery.com.au
www.timboondistillery.com/
They produce pot distilled single malt whisky.

TRIPTYCH DISTILLERY
Yarra Valley, Victoria
Australia
Email: info@triptychdistillery.com.au
www.triptychdistillery.com.au
They are planning to produce small batch whiskey made from local grain.

VICTORIA VALLEY DISTILLERY
Building 136
181 Larkin St.
Essendon Fields, Victoria 3041
Australia
Tel: +61 3 9005 4420
Email: Built into their website
www.victoriavalley.com.au
Established in 2007 in part by Lark Distillery, they are currently producing whisky that is maturing in a variety of oak barrels.

WILD SWAN DISTILLING COMPANY
10581 West Swan Rd.
Henley Brook, Western Australia 6055
Australia Tel: +61 08 9296 6656
Email: Built into their website
www.wildswandistillery.com.au
Established in 2002 they are currently maturing their whisky which will be sold as Wild Swan Whisky.

WILLIAM MCHENRY AND SONS DISTILLERY
229 Radnor Rd.
Port Arthur, Tasmania 7182
Australia
Tel: +61 03 6250 2533
Established in 2011, they intend to produce single batch spirits, including "Three Capes Whisky."

NEW ZEALAND

SOUTHERN DISTILLING COMPANY
Stafford St.
Timaro, New Zealand
Tel: +64 03 686 6515
Email: spirits@xtra.co.nz
www.hokonuiwhiskey.com

The Southern Distilling Company, the world's southernmost distillery, produces a legal moonshine called "Old Hokonui," "The Coaster" Single Malt, "The MacKenzie" Blended Malt, and "Potin Illegal Whisky" which is distilled from malted barley and treacle, a type of cane syrup.

SOUTHERN GRAIN SPIRITS NZ LTD
Physical Address:
94 Peraki St.
Kaiapoi
Cantebury
New Zealand
Postal Address:
PO Box 81
Kaiapoi
Canterbury
New Zealand
Tel: +64 03 327 6389
Email: spirits@southerngrainspirits.co.nz
www.southerngrainspirits.co.nz

They produce Shepherd's Whisky which is a blend of imported five year old Malt Whisky and distilled Grain Spirit.

SOUTHERN PACIFIC DISTILLERY
258 Wakefield Quay
Nelson
New Zealand
Tel: +64 03 546 6822
Email: brian@roaringforties.co.nz
www.roaringforties.co.nz

Founded in 1982, they produce, among other things, Roaring Forties Single Malt Whisky.

REISETBAUER | AUSTRIA

REISETBAUER Products include a 7-year old single malt blend, matured in ex-Chardonnay and Austrian sweet wine casks, and a 12-year old whisky. [page 29]

EUROPE

Wolfram Ortner | Austria

Wolfram Ortner This business, which specializes in various luxury items, produces a whisky called "Nockland." [page 29]

AUSTRIA

BRENNEREI HIEBL
Reichhub 36
3350 Haag
Austria
Tel: +43 7434 42114
Email: schnaps@die-schnapsidee.at
www.die-schnapsidee.at
The George Hiebl Distillery produces a Malted Oat Whisky, Malted Rye Whisky and Malted Spelt Whisky.

BRENNEREI WEIDENAUER
Leopolds 6
3623 Kottes
Austria
Tel: +43(0) 2873 7276
Email: info@weidenauer.at
www.weidenauer.at
Whiskies they produce include the Oat Whisky, Spelt Whisky, and Malted Spelt Whiskey.

BROGER PRIVATBRENNEREI
Dammweg 43
6833 Klaus
Austria
Tel: +43(0) 5523 53546
Email: office@broger.info
www.broger.info
Brothers Bruno and Eugen Broger have been producing whisky since 2008. Their current range of whiskies include Riebelmais, a whisky made from a special corn variety and three Single Malt whiskies: the first is medium smoked; the second is heavily peated and called Burn Out; the third is called Triple Cask, because it has been aged in ex-Bourbon, ex-Sherry and ex-Madeira casks.

DACHSTEIN–DESTILLERIE
Mandlbergweg 11
5550 Radstadt
Austria
Tel: +43(0) 6454 7660
Email: info@mandlberggut.com
www.mandlberggut.com/
Whisky production started here in 2007. Their Rock-Whisky is a classic single malt which has been aged in barrels made from local Austrian oak and ex-Sherry-casks and stored in a specially dug earthen cellar.

DESTILLERIE HARALD KECKEIS
Torkelgässele 3
6830 Rankweil
Austria
Tel: +43(0) 66411 38868
Email: harald@destillerie-keckeis.at
www.destillerie-keckeis.at
They are currently producing a single malt spirit and selling it direct to consumers in 10 and 30 liter barrels. This allows the customer to taste the spirit at will and taste the changes as it matures into whiskey.

DESTILLERIE HERMANN PFANNER
Alte Landstraße 10
6923 Lauterach
Austria
Tel: +43(0) 5574 6720460
Email: walter.pfanner@pfanner.com
www.pfanner-weine.com/
This drinks company, located only a mile or two from Lake Constance, started whisky production in 2005. Their single malt matures in ex-Sherry and other sweet wine barrels. Since opening in 2005 only a few bottlings have been released but their production of about 10,000 liters of whisky per year is promising.

DESTILLERIE ROGNER
Roiten 13
3911 Rappottenstein
Austria
Tel: +43(0) 2828 8505
Email: rogner.roiten@aon.at
www.destillerie-rogner.at
This family distillery is in its second generation of operation and produces fruit spirits and three whiskies. Their Whisky 3/3 is made from three different cereals though they do not specify what they are. Thier Whisky No. 2 is made from malted and un-malted barley some of which has been smoked over peat. They also produce Rye Whisky No. 13.

EDELBRENNEREI FRANZ KOSTENZER
Achensee Straße 22
6212 Maurach,
Austria
Tel: +43(0) 05243 5795
Email: info@schnaps-achensee.at
www.schnaps-achensee.at
This family distillery opened in 1998 and began producing fruit spirits. In 2005 they began producing grain spirits that would age into whisky. They now offer two versions of their four years old Whisky Alpin: a Rye & Malt Whisky bottled at 40% abv and a Grain Whisky Hafer (oat whisky) bottled at 44% abv.

The Owl Distillery | Belgium

Owl Distillery Distiller Etienne Bouillon produces a three year old whisky called "The Belgian Owl" Single Malt Belgium Whisky, aged in 1st fill bourbon casks. [page 31]

LAGLER GMBH
Hotelgasse 1
7543 Kukmirn
Austria
Tel: +43(0) 3328 32003
Email: info@lagler.cc
www.lagler.cc

Along with a wide variety of fruit spirits they also produce three whiskies: Lagler's Pannonia Blend 38.5% abv, Lagler's Pannonia grain malt 40% abv, and Lagler's Best Grain Burgenland 43% abv.

LAVA-BRAEU
Auersbach 130
8330 Feldbach
Austria
Tel: +43(0) 3152 8575 300
Email: office@lavabraeu.at
www.brisky.at

This brewery started whisky production in 2003. Currently, there are three whiskies in their portfolio: Genesis, is a single malt bottled at cask strength and entirely matured in a mulberry cask; Brisky, is a classic single malt; and Woazky, is made from corn with a small proportion of malted barley. The last two are both aged in oak barrels.

MARILLENHOF DESTILLERIE KAUSL
Oetz 16
3622 Muehldorf
Austria
Tel: +43(0) 676 380 94 65
Email: info@marillenhof.at
www.wachauer-whisky.at

This family business, known for producing apricot eau-de-vies, has been making grain whiskies for the last 15 years. Their wheat, spelt, barley, oat and rye whiskies are mainly matured in small Austrian oak barrels.

REISETBAUER
Zum Kirchdorfergut 1
4062 Axberg
Austria
Tel: + 43(0) 7221 63690
Email: office@reisetbauer.at
www.reisetbauer.at

Founded in 1994, the Hans Reisetbauer distillery's products include a 7-year old single malt blend, matured in ex-Chardonnay and Austrian sweet wine casks, as well as a 12-year old single malt whisky.

WALDVIERTLER GRANITDESTILLERIE
Hollenbach Nr. 117
3830 Waidhofen/Thaya
Austria
Tel: +43(0) 664 432 40 03
Email: granitdestillerie@aon.at
www.granitdestillerie.at

Guenther Mayer began producing whisky in 2007. Today he is offering different whiskies from a variety of malted ingredients like barley, spelt and rye. Each has a standard bottling at 42% abv and a stronger bottling at 54% abv. Peat freaks will enjoy his single malt made from "re-peated" malt, which is soaked in water for a second time and then dried over a fire of local peat.

WALDVIERTLER ROGGENHOF
Whisky-Eriebniswelt J. Haider GmbH
Johann und Monika Haider
3664 Roggenreith 3
Austria
Tel: +43(0) 2874 7496
Email: haider@roggenhof.at
www.roggenhof.at

Established in 1995, they claim to be Austria's first whisky distillery. Currently they have a range of six whiskies: Rye Whisky JH, Pure Rye Malt Whisky JH, Special Pure Rye Malt Whisky JH "Nougat," Single Malt Whisky JH, Special Single Malt Whisky JH "Karamell," and Rye Whisky JH Liqueur "Northern Dream."

WEUTZ
St Nikolai Nr. 6
8505 St. Nikolai im Sausal
Nikolai im Sausal
Austria
Tel: +43(0) 3185 34440
Email: distillerie@weutz.at
www.weutz.at

Destillerie Weutz currently produces over 12 whiskies distilled from wheat, barley, and spelt, rested in French Limousin and Allier oak.

WOLFRAM ORTNER
Untertscherner Weg 3
9546 Bad Kleinkirchheim
Austria
Tel: +43 4240 760
Email: info@wob.at
www.wob.at

This business, which specializes in various luxury items, produces a whisky called "Nockland."

ØRBÆK BRYGGERI | DENMARK

ØRBÆK BRYGGERI will be releasing two whiskies: Fionia Smoked Whisky and Isle of Fiona, both aged in ex-Tennessee whiskey and ex-sherry casks. [page 32]

BELGIUM

BROUWERIZ HET ANKER
Guido Gezellenlaan 49
B-2800 Mechelen
Belgium
Tel: + 32(0)15 287 147
Email: info@hetanker.be
www.hetanker.be
Production began in 2003 and in 2007 Het Anker has released two lots of its Gouden Carolus Single Malt Whisky, distilled from Gouden Carolus Tripel beer. They are currently expecting their next batch of whisky to finish maturing and ready for bottling in 2013.

GRAANSTOKERIJ FILLIERS
Leernsesteenweg 5
9800 Deinze
Belgium
Tel: +32 (0)9 386 12 64
Email: info@filliers.be
www.filliers.be
Fillers Grain Distillery has a long history of making Gin but they also produce Goldys 10-year old Belgian Double Still Whisky and Goldys Owners Reserve.

THE OWL DISTILLERY
Rue Sainte Anne 94
4460 Grâce-Hollogne
Belgium
Tel: + 32 (0) 4 247 38 14
Email: etienne.bouillon@belgianwhisky.com
www.belgianwhisky.com
Founded in 2004, distiller Etienne Bouillon produces "The Belgian Owl" Single Malt Belgium Whisky which is aged in 1st fill bourbon casks and bottled at 46% abv as well as Cask Strength. They also produce a Belgium Single Malt Spirit, in a "Not Aged," 12-month and 24 month bottlings at 46% abv.

CZECH REPUBLIC

KOJETIN DISTILLERY
Olomouc 772 48
Hodolanska 32 PSC 772 48
Czech Republic
Tel: +420 641 753 111
Email: kojetin@lihovar.com
www.lihovar.com
Owned by Lihovar, Kojetin distillery produces neutral grain spirits for use by other alcohol beverage companies.

RUDOLF JELINEK A.S.
Razav 472
763 12 Vizovice
Czech Republic
Email: rjelinek@rjelinek.cz
www.rjelinek.cz
They produce Gold Cock, a 3-year and a 12-year single malt whisky made from Moravian barley. They claim their distilling heritage goes back to the 1880s which survived nationalization during the communist era and reemerged after independence.

STOCK PLZEN
Palírenská 641/2
326 00, Plzeň – Božkov
Czech Republic
Tel: +420 378 081 111
Email: Built into their website
www.stock.cz/en
They produce Printer's Whisky which is a peated Scottish style whisky aged for 6 years before bottling.

DENMARK

DESTILLERIET BRAUNSTEIN
Carlsensvej 5 – 4600 Köge
Koge, Sjaelland
Denmark
Tel: +45 7020 4468
Email: mail@braunstein.dk
www.braunstein.dk
Braunstein, billed as Denmark's first micro distillery, bottles a very wide variety of whiskies. Braunstein Whisky Edition No. 1, was matured in ex-oloroso sherry casks, while other editions have used ex-bourbon or new French oak.

FARY LOCHAN DESTILLERI
Co/Smedevej 15, Farre
DK – 7323 Give
Tel: +45 7573 3330
Email: info@farylochan.dk
www.farylochan.com
Established in 2009, this Jutland distillery anticipates releasing its first whisky in 2013 or 2014.

NORDISK BRAENDERI
Hjortdalvej 227,
9690 Fjerritslev
Denmark
Tel: +45 9821 7080, +45 2093 3656
Email: andersbilgram@me.com
www.nordiskbraenderi.dk
They began distilling whisky in 2010 and their first release will be bottled at 59.6% abv after three years in a Bowmore barrel. The whisky was made

from locally grown, organic Imperial malted barley which was lightly smoked. They also have four other whiskies maturing in four different size and type barrels. While their second release is planed for January 2014, future bottlings will be released annually until they grow beyond their 2 barrels-a-year production capacity.

ØRBÆK BRYGGERI
Orbaek Bryggeri
Assensvej 38
5853 Orbaek
Orbaek, Funen (Island)
Denmark
Tel: +45 6533 2111
Email: info@oerbaek-bryggeri.nu
www.oerbaek-bryggeri.nu

Ørbæk Bryggeri, a brewery that began distilling in 2007. They will be releasing two whiskies in the summer of 2012: Fionia Smoked Whisky and Isle of Fiona. Their whiskies are made from organic malted barley and aged in ex-Tennessee whiskey and ex-sherry casks.

STAUNING
Stauningvej 38
6900 Skjern
Denmark
Tel: +45 4244 2122
Email: inf@stauningwhisky.dk
www.stauningwhisky.dk

Founded in 2006, this Danish distillery currently produces three expressions of its whisky: Peated Reserve, Traditional Reserve, and a Rye Whisky. They also have a number of experiments that they are considering bottling in the future as special edition releases.

TROLDEN DISTILLERY
Olaf Ryes Gade 7m DK-6000 Kolding
Denmark
Tel: +45 2845 0755
Email: info@trolden.com
www.trolden.com/distillery.html

Founded in 2011 as an extension of Trolden Brewery, they are planning on producing whisky in the Scottish style: distilled twice and aged in ex-bourbon casks, some peated and some unpeated.

VINGÅRDEN LILLE GADEGÅRD
Jesper Paulsen
Sondre Landevej 63
DK-3720 Aakirkeby
Denmark
Tel: + 45 21 62 88 57
Email: A7@a7.dk
www.a7.dk

The only whisky produced at this distillery and winery is Lille Gadegard Bornholmsk Whisky. They are currently selling their second vintage bottled in 2010 after three years in oak.

FINLAND

PANIMORAVINTOLA BEER HUNTER'S
Antinkatu 11
28100 Pori
Finland
Tel: +358 2 641 55 99
www.beerhunters.fi

They began producing whisky in 2001 and they have been selling their Old Buck whisky since 2004.

TEERENPELI
Teerenpeli Malt Whisky Distillery
Hämeenkatu 19, Lahti
Finland
Tel: +358 500 830 458
Email: mail@teerenpeli.com
www.teerenpeli.com

The single malt expressions produced at Teerenpeli include 3, 4, 5, and 6-year old whiskies matured in ex sherry and bourbon casks.

FRANCE

DISTILLERIE BERTRAND
3 Rue du Marechal Leclerc
BP 21 67350 Uberach, Alsace
France
Tel: +33 (0)3 88 07 70 83
Email: contact@distillerie-bertrand.com
www.distillerie-bertrand.com

This distillery in the northern part of Alsace produces two whiskies: a blend called Uberach Single Malt Alsace Whisky, which uses ex-Banyuls fortified wine casks and new wood; and Uberach Single Cask Alsace Whisky, aged in Banyuls barrels for 3 years.

DISTILLERIE F. MEYER
18 Rue Saint-Gilles
67220 Hohwarth
France
Tel: +33 (0)3 88 85 61 44
Email: distillerie.meyer@wanadoo.fr
www.distillerie-meyer.fr
This eau-de-vie distillery also produces two whiskies. Meyer's Pur Malt, is 100% malted barley, distilled twice and aged in oak barrels for 3 years. Meyer's Blend Supérieur, is a blend of malt and grain whiskies aged in oak that once contained sweet wine.

DISTILLERIE KAERILIS
4 Rue Amiral Willaumez
56360 Le Palais
Belle Isle en Mer
France
Tel: +33(0) 297 312820; +33(0) 619 978698
Email: info@kaeriliswhisky.com
www.kaeriliswhisky.com
Distillerie Kaerilis is on the largest French island off the coast of Brittany in the Bay of Biscay. They produce five different expressions of whisky all of which are un-chill filtered and bottled from single casks. Their whiskies are: Premier Eté à Belle-Isle (First Summer Belle-Isle); Ster Vrtz No. 9, a peated whisky made with peat from Belle-Isle; Rêve d'Azur (Rivera Dreams), a 12 year old single malt aged in sherry and rum casks and bottled at 45% abv; Une Etoile en Mer (A Star at Sea), an 11 year old whisky finished in sherry casks and bottled at 56.8% abv; Le Grand Dérangement (The Great Upheaval) and A l'Aube du Grand Dérangement (At the Dawn of the Great Upheaval) are a 15 year old whisky bottled at 43% and 57% abv respectively.

DISTILLERIE DES MENHIRS
7 Hent Sant Philibert
29700 Plomelin, Bretagne
Brittany, France
Tel: +33 (0)2 98 94 23 68
Email: contact@distillerie.fr
www.distillerie.fr
This unique distillery in Brittany distills a whisky made from buckwheat. It produces two expressions of its whisky, Eddu Silver, and Eddu Grey Rock, all aged in French oak. "Eddu" means buckwheat in the local Breton dialect.

DISTILLERIE DE MONSIEUR BALTHAZAR
8, Place de la Republique
BP 11 03190 Herisson
France
Tel: +33 (0)4 70 06 85 57
Email: Website states that there is no email contact for the distillery
www.whisky-hedgehog.fr
Mr. Balthazar's distillery produces Hedgehog Straight Whisky Bourbonnais, made with 65% organic corn, malted barley, and rye, and aged for three years in Tronçais oak. Balthazar also produces a number of liqueurs using the whisky as a base and flavored with a different herbs and fruits.

DOMAINE MAVELA
U licettu
20270 Aléria
Corsica, France
Tel: +33 (0)4 95 56 60 30
Email: boutique@domaine-mavela.com
www.domaine-mavela.com
P & M Whiskies (Pietra and Mavela) on the French island of Corsica are the made from the marriage of the Pietra brewery and Domaine Mavela, who distills the whisky. Products include P&M Blend, P&M Superieur, and P&M Single Malt aged 7 years. Their casks, which are only lightly toasted and sourced from the Tronçet forest, are first filled with white wine or Muscat.

FERME-BRASSERIE LA CHAPELLA
76780 La Chapelle Saint-Ouen
France
Tel: +33 (0)2 35 09 21 54
Email: brasserie@northmaen.com
www.northmaen.com
Founded in 1997, Northmæn is primarily a farm brewery but they also produce Thor Boyo whisky which has been aged for at least three years and bottled at 42% abv.

GILBERT HOLL DISTILLERIE
Route de Sainte-Marie-aux-Mines 68150
Ribeauville
Alsace, France
Tel: +33 (0)3 89 73 70 34
Email: info@gilbertholl.com
www.gilbertholl.com
Both a brewery and distillery Gilbert Holl produces the first Alsatian Whisky called Loc' Holl. He has done three bottlings of a 7, 8, and 10-year old whisky produced from a blend of several different barley malts.

Blaue Maus | Germany

Blaue Maus This is the first single malt distillery in Bavaria, offering seven different single malts. [page 36]

GLANN AR MOR
2 allée des Embruns
22610 Larmor-Pleubian
Brittany, France
Email: info@glannarmor.com
www.glannarmor.com
Dubbed as "the Celtic distillery with a Breton heart," this seaside distillery first produced 99 bottles of an unpeated, ex-bourbon barrel-aged whisky called Glann ar Mor Taol Esa. Currently the distillery produces and sells their whisky to individual customers by the cask, which is aged at least three years in ex-burgundy wine casks.

GRALLET-DUPIC
16 rue du Capitaine Durand
54290 Rozelieures
Lorraine, France
Tel: +33 (0)3 83 72 32 26
Email: hubert.grallet@wanadoo.fr
www.maisondelamirabelle.com
Primarily a distiller of Eau de Vie, they are the first whisky producer in Lorraine. Their G.Rozelieures (Single Malt) Whisky de Lorraine is aged for at least three years in ex-wine barrels from southern Spain.

GUILLON
Hameau de Vertuelle
51150 Louvois
France
Tel: +33 (0)3 26 51 87 50
Email: contact@distillerie-guillon.com
www.distillerie-guillon.com
Distillerie Guillon makes a range of single malt and blended whiskies, including Guillon No. 1. The distillery prefers to mature its whiskies in ex wine casks, such as Sauterne or Banyuls.

LIQUEURS FISSELIER
56 Rue de Verger
35571 Chantepie
Brittany, France
Tel: +33 (0)2 99 41 00 00
Email: contact@jacques-fisselier.com
www.jacques-fisselier.com
Although this Brittany distillery primarily produces liqueurs, it also makes two blended, 100% "grain" whiskies: Gwenroc Whiskey Breton and Whiskey de Bretagne.

WAMBRECHIES
1, Rue de la Distillerie
59118 Wambrechies
France
Tel: +33 (0)3 20 14 91 91
Email: info@wambrechies.com
www.wambrechies.com
This genever distillery produces two whiskies, a 3-year old and an 8-year old Wambrechies Whisky Single Malt.

WARENGHEM
Route de Guingamp
22300 Lannion
Brittany, France
Tel: +33 (0)2 96 37 00 08
Email: info@distillerie-warenghem.com
www.distillerie-warenghem.com
Located in Brittany, Warenghem makes two series of its whisky: Armorik, represented by 4 different Single Malt Whiskies that vary in age, finishing barrels, and bottling strength; and three blended whiskies that have a 50-50, or 25-75% malt whisky to grain whisky ratios.

GERMANY

BELLERHOF BRENNEREI
Berghof 1a
73277 Owen
Baden-Württemberg
Germany
Tel: +49 (7021) 51892
Email: Thomas.Dannenmann@t-online.de
www.bellerhof-brennerei.com
Their first whisky run of rye and wheat distillate started in 1990, and was aged for 3 years in German Oak. Today the mash consist of barley, rye, and wheat and is aged in both German oak and ex-Bourbon barrels from the United States. Their current bottling of whisky is 8 years old.

BERGHOF RABEL
Berghof
73277 Owen-Teck
Baden-Wurttemberg,
Germany
Tel: +49 (07021) 861961
Email: info@berghof-rabel.de
www.berghof-rabel.de
Founded in 1958, this schnapps distillery also produce two whiskies and a whisky liquor. Schwäbischer whiskey is called a single grain whisky though it is made from a blend of 85% wheat and 15% barley; their Albdinkel whisky is made from spelt and aged in German oak; their whisky liqueur is sweetened with honey.

BIRKENHOF BRENNEREI
Auf dem Birkenhof
57647 Nistertal
Rhineland-Palatinate
Germany
Tel: +49 (0) 2661 982 040
Email: info@birkenhof-brennerei.de
www.birkenhof-brennerei.de

They first began production in 2002 and have focused on producing high quality whisky from German rye. Their whisky, Fading Hill, which is named for a nearby basalt formation that is disappearing due to mining, consists of 90% rye and 10% malted barley, is aged for 5 ½ years in sherry casks and bottled at cask strength. They are also producing whiskies made from other grains and matured in a variety of casks. They have a large tasting room with a glass floor that looks down onto their whisky barrels and they have been releasing a new whisky each April.

BLAUE MAUS
Bamberger Str. 2
91330 Eggolsheim
Bavaria
Germany
Tel: +49 (09848) 7461
Email: info@fleischmann-whisky.de
www.fleischmann-whisky.de

Founded in 1983, this is the first single malt distillery in Bavaria, offering several single cask bottlings of Single Malt Whisky.

BOSCH EDELBRAND
Kirchheimer Straße 43
73252 Lenningen
Baden-Württemberg
Germany
Tel: +49(07026) 7881
Email: info@bosch-edelbrand.de
www.bosch-edelbrand.de

Founded in 1948 by the current distiller's grandfather, they produce JR Whisky which is made from locally-grown malted spelt.

BRENNEREI ALOIS SCHRAML
Pfarrgasse 22
92681 Erbendorf
Bavaria
Germany
Tel: +49 (09682) 881
Email: info@brennerei-schraml.de
www.brennerei-schraml.de

They produce a wide variety of spirits and liqueurs including Stonewood 1818 Single Grain Whisky. It is aged for 10 years and each bottle is numbered.

BRENNEREI BISCHOF
Hauptstraße 1
97797 Wartmannsroth
Bavaria
Germany
Tel: +49 (09737) 1318
Email: info@brennerei-bischof.de
brennerei-bischof.de

Primarily a producer of fruit brandies they have been producing Rhöner Whisky from wheat and barley in an expanded and updated still house since 1995.

BRENNEREI GRUEL
Neue Strasse 26 73277 Owen
Baden-Wurttemberg
Germany
Tel: +49 (07021) 59985
Email: info@manufaktur-gruel.de
www.manufaktur-gruel.de

Among other products they make Tecker Single Grain Whisky which is made from 85% wheat and 15% malted barley. In Germany it is understood that the term "Single Grain" refers to a spirit made mostly of one grain with 15% malted barley added for starch conversion. They use organic grains and age the spirit in ex-Bourbon barrels for five years before bottling. They also produce a whisky from smoked and roasted malts and aged in sherry casks called, Sherry Cask Single Malt Whisky. They have also produced a number of special edition whiskies.

BRENNEREI HÖHLER
Kirchgasse 3
65326 Aarbergen
Hessia
Germany
Tel: +49 (06120) 1321
Email: holger@brennerei-hoehler.de
www.brennerei-hoehler.de

This whisky, or "whesskey," as it is called at the distillery, comes in four styles- Hessian Blended Whisky, Hessian Single Malt Whisky, Hessian Corn Whisky, and a Whesskey liqueur.

BRENNEREI LIEBL
Gerhard Liebl
Jahnstraße 11-15, 93444
Bad Kötzting
Germany
Tel: +49 (09941) 1321
Email: liebl-baerwurz@t-online.de
www.coillmor.de or baerwurzerei-liebl.de

They make a single malt whisky from Bavarian malt and age it a minimum of 3 years in a variety of barrels. They produce a number of whiskies under the label Coillmór— the Gaelic word for big forest which refers to the heavily forested area surrounding the distillery.

BRENNEREI LUDWIG FABER
Buechelstrasse 20
54668 Ferschweiler
Germany
Tel. +49(0) 6523 245
Email: brennerei@faber-eifelbrand.de
www.faber-eifelbrand.de

The family owned distillery began making spirits from local fruit in 1949. In 2003 father and son produced their first single malt whisky. It aged for 6 years in American White Oak barrels and was released in 2009. Their spirit "Whisky aus der Eifel" is named after its home in the extraordinary volcanic region close to the Luxembourg border.

BRENNEREI RODER
Buerglesteige 31
73433 Aalen – Wasseralfingen
Germany
Tel: +49(0) 7361 971 625
Email: info@brennerei-roder.de
www.brennerei-roder.de

The distillery is 3rd generation family owned and operated by Frank Roder. He first produced a wheat whisky in 2000. The 4 year old, ex-Bourbon barrel matured "Frank's Suebisch Whisky" was named after a group of people that lived in the area during roman times. Roder has also contributed to Hala-Whisky, a blend of three 7-year-old grain whisky barrels from local producers (www.hala-whisky.de). His nicely decorated distillery shop, Destillathek, is in the center of the town and offers all of his spirits for sale

BRENNEREI SIGEL
Obere Strasse 11
73265 Dettingen
Baden-Württemberg
Germany
Tel: +49 (0 70 21) 5 33 48

Also a brandy distillery, they make a whisky called Malt and Grain, which is a blend of wheat and barley spirits, aged for 6 years. They only produce about 100 small bottles a year.

BRENNEREI VOLKER THEURER
Jesinger Hauptstr. 55/57 70202 Tübingen-Unterjesingen
Baden-Württemberg
Germany
Tel: +49 (7073) 5159
Email: lamm-tuebingen@t-online.de
www.lamm-tuebingen.de

This hotel, restaurant and distillery makes a variety of fruit brandies, as well as grain schnapps. They produce Saint John which is a Swabian Single Malt Whisky bottled from a single barrel; Ammertal Whisky which is a blend of single malt and grain whisky that is aged at least three years and Ammertal Gold which is a whisky liqueur with honey and vanilla.

DESTILLERIE KAMMER-KIRSCH GMBH
Hardtstraße 37
76185 Karlsruhe
Baden-Württemberg
Germany
Tel: +49 (7219) 55510
Email: info@kammer-kirsch.de
http://www.kammer-kirsch.de

Founded in 1909, this historic distillery, in partnership with the over 200-year old Rothaus Brewery, produces Rothaus Black Forest Single Malt Whisky.

FEINBRENNEREI SIMON'S
Doersthof 4
63755 Alzenau-Michelbach
Germany
Tel: +49(0) 6023 507 21 91
Email: spirit@feinbrenner.eu
www.feinbrenner.eu

Severin Simon began producing his Bavarian Pure Pot Still Whiskey in 1998. This whisky is modeled after an Irish recipe with a large fraction of raw barley from his own fields and a smaller portion of malted barley from a local maltster. He has recently upgraded his distilling license, from an annual limit of 300 liters pure alcohol, to an unlimited amount of spirits produced under bond.

FINCH WHISKY
Aicherstr. 7
89191 Nellingen
Baden-Württemberg
Germany
Tel: +49 (07337) 969699
Email: info@finch-whisky.de
www.finch-whisky.de/home.php

They make a five year old Schwäbischer Highland whisky which is made from their farm grown spelt and wheat mixed with 15% malted barley. The spirit is produced about 600 meters above sea level, matured in used wine barrels from Greece and a small portion is finished in Port barrels. As of April 2012 the distillery installed a new 2000 liters still, which is the largest in any of the German speaking countries.

Brennerei Holle | Switzerland

Brennerei Holle Hagen's Best Swiss Single Malt Whisky is distilled three times and then rested in bourbon barrels. [page 44]

EDELOBSTBRENNEREI ZIEGLER
Gerb. J. & M. Ziegler GmbH
Hauptstraße 26
97896 Freundenberg
Baden-Württemberg
Germany
Tel: +49 (09375) 92880
Email: info@brennerei-ziegler.de
www.brennerei-ziegler.de

Founded in 1865, this distillery produces a wide array of fruit brandies, liqueurs and Aureum 1865 Single Malt Whisky. The whisky is made from locally-grown grain which is malted and mashed by a nearby brewery. The spirit is matured in lightly toasted oak and chestnut barrels from France and then finished in ex-Bourbon barrels from the US.

HAMMERSCHMIEDE SPIRITUOSEN
Elsbach 11A
37449 Zorge
Lower Saxony
Germany
Tel: +49 (05586) 8282
Email: info@hammerschmiede.de
www.hammerschmiede-spirituosen.de

Their whisky production began in 2002 with the first bottlings in 2005. Their Glen Els Whisky is made from malted barley and aged in a dozen different barrel types for up to five years. Their whisky is hand bottled usually from single casks without dilution.

KLEINBRENNEREI FITZKE
Riedstraße 18
79336 Herbolzheim-Broggingen
Baden-Württemberg
Germany
Tel: +49(07643) 1523
Email: info@kleinbrennerei-fitzke.de
www.kleinbrennerei-fitzke.de

This distillery began producing whisky in 2004 and offers a wide variety of malted and unmalted whiskies made from barley, wheat, rye, triticale (a wheat rye hybrid), corn, spelt, buckwheat, oats, rice, millet, emmer and einkorn (both a variety of hulled wheat). All their whiskies start off the first six months in new toasted 30 liter Slovenian oak barrels and then the rest of the time in previously used whisky barrels.

MÄRKISCHE SPEZIÄLIATENBRENNEREI
In der Asmecke 12
58091 Hagen
North Rhine-Westphalia
Germany
Tel:+49 (02337) 485894
Email: info@msb-hagen.de
www.maerkische-spezialitaeten-brennerei.de

Along with fruit spirits this distillery produces Single Malt Whisky Tronje von Hagen bottled at 55% abv, and three bottlings of their new barley spirit: Single Malt New Make Tronje von Hagen Clear bottled at 55% abv; Single Malt New Make Tronje von Hagen barrel aged (less than 3 years) bottled at 46% and 55% abv and a Whiskylikör Tronje von Hagen bottled at 25% abv. Their barrels house is climate controlled to 10 °C (50 °F) at 100% humidity.

OBSTHOF AM BERG
Auf der Hohlmauer 2
65830 Kriftel
Hessia
Germany
Tel: +49(06192) 42961
Email: obsthof@obsthof-am-berg.de
www.gilors.de

This distillery produces two whiskies each aged for at least three years, the first whisky in Sherry barrels and the second in Port casks.

OBST-KORN BRENNEREI ZAISER
Hussengasse 1
73257 Köngen
Baden-Württemberg
Germany
Tel: +49 (7024) 82224
Email: info@obstbrennerei.de
www.obstbrennerei.de

Among their assortment of fruit brandies they also produce a small amount of whisky. Zaiser Schwäbischen Whisky made from wheat and barley, the distillate is stored in German Oak, Hungarian Oak, and Sherry Casks before being blended together and bottled. Their Zaiser Schwäbischen Roasted Grain Whisky is made from hand-roasted wheat and aged for three years in Hungarian Oak. They also make a Single Cask Whisky by aging their Schwäbischen Whisky for an extra six years in a 30-year old, 144 liter apple cider cask before bottling it a 40% abv.

PREUSSISCHE WHISKYDESTILLERIE
Am Gutshof 3
16278 Mark Landin
Brandenburg
Germany
Tel: +49(033335) 318950
Email: info@preussischerwhisky.de
www.preussischerwhisky.de

Operated by one of the few women maters distillers in Germany, Cornelia Bohn is producing Preussischer Whisky which is made from a variety of barley malts included roasted malt and malted barley smoked over beechwood. The whisky is aged for three months in American white oak and then in German Spessart oak barrels for a total of three years. Each bottle is hand numbered and filled from a single barrel at cask strength.

SLYRS DESTILLERIE GMBH & CO. KG
Bayrischzeller Strasse 13
83727 Schliersee
Bavaria
Germany
Tel: +49 (08026) 9222795
Email: info@slyrs.de
www.slyrs.de

Currently they are the largest distillery in Germany with annual sales of about 60,000 bottles. Their flagship Slyrs Bavarian Single Malt is made in part with malted barley that has been dried over beechwood smoke and matured for 3 years in American white oak casks. They also make a whisky liqueur with honey and vanilla as well as Cask Strength bottlings.

SPREEWÄLDER FEINBRAND
Dorfstraße 56
15910 Schlepzig
Brandenburg
Germany
Tel: +49 (035472) 659142
Email: spreewaldbrennerei@t-online.de
www.spreewaldbrennerei.de

They began producing single malt spirits in 2004 with the first bottling of their Sloupisti Single Malt Whisky in 2008. Their whisky is released in numbered editions both at 40% abv and cask strength. Their next whisky is expected to be bottled in 2014.

STEINHAUSER GMBH
Raiffeisen Strasse 23
88079 Kressbronn
Baden-Württemberg
Germany
Tel: +49 (07543) 8061
Email: mail@weinkellerei-steinhauser.de
www.weinkellerei-steinhauser.de

This winery and distillery began producing whisky in 2008. They have released their first bottling of Brigantia Whisky which is a single malt whisky made near Lake Constance in Southwest Germany. Their whisky was produced on a restored still from 1890.

WEINGUT MÖSSLEIN
Untere Dorfstrasse 8,
97509 Zeilitzheim
Bavaria,
Germany
Tel: +49 (09381) 1506
Email: info@weingeister.de
www.weingeister.de

They produce Fränkischer Whisky which is aged for five years in used wine barrels from their own winery. They only produce about 100 bottles a year.

LIECHTENSTEIN

BRENNEREI TELSER
Dorfstrasse 67 9495 Triesen
Liechtenstein
Tel: +423 392 29 45
Email: telser@brennerei-telser.com
www.brennerei-telser.com

Besides brandy, this distillery also produces Telsington Single Cask Malt Whisky. The whisky is matured in used wine barrels and bottled each year from single casks.

DISTILLERIE DIEDENACKER
9A Rue Puert
5433 Niederdonven
Luxembourg
Tel: +352(0) 26 747 108
Email: duhrcam@pt.lu
www.diedenacker.lu

Camille and Mariette Duhr-Merges are the owners of this farm distillery close to the German boarder. They mainly use home-grown fruits to produce first class eau-de-vies. In 2005 they distilled the first Luxembourg whisky from their own rye with a small proportion of malt. After it matured for 5 years in oak barrels, that once held local wines, it was bottled in 2010 and sold out immediately. Since then all their whiskies, which are highly sought-after, are released annually and usually sell out before they are even bottled. As of June 2013 they are still the only whisky producers in Luxembourg.

NETHERLANDS

R. GORTER & ZN BV
Zijlstraat 2
3111 PS Schiedam
Netherlands
Tel: +32 (0)104 091000
They produce Maltky Blended Whisky which is a blend of Scotch and Dutch grain spirits.

US HEIT DISTILLERY
Snekerstraat 43
8701 XC Bolsward
Friesland
Netherlands
Tel: +31 (0)515 577449
Email: contact@usheitdistillery.nl
www.usheitdistillery.nl
US Heit produces a 3-year old whisky, which goes under the name "Frysk Hynder." The whisky is aged in ex cognac, sherry and wine casks.

ZUIDAM DISTILLERS
Smederijstraat 5
5111 PT Baarle Nassau
Netherlands
Tel: +31 13 507 8470
Email: info@zuidam-distillers.com
www.zuidam-distillers.com
As one of the last independent distilleries in the Netherlands, Zuidam sells a 5-year old single malt, known as Millstone Dutch Single Malt Whisky. The distillery uses small barrels of new American oak, as well as ex-Bourbon, and ex-Sherry casks for maturation. They also produce two 8-year old whiskies, one aged primarily in French oak and the other in American oak. Lastly they produce a 5-year old Dutch Rye Whisky.

NORWAY

AGDER BRENNERI
Østerhus Næringspark
4891 Grimstad
Norway
Tel: +47 37 04 01 44 / 37 25 60 80
Email: post@agderbrenneri.no
www.agderbrenneri.no
Primarily a producer of Akevitt, whisky production began in 2009 and they planned to introduce Norway's first Single Malt Whisky in November 2012. Their new spirit has been aging in old oloroso sherry casks and they are expecting to bottle about 600 350ml bottles. Their goal is to reach about 20,000 bottles and age their whisky between three and five years.

KLOSTERGÅRDEN HÅNDBRYGGERI
7633 Frosta
Tautra, Norway
Tel: +47 7480 8533
Email: annemarthalia@gmail.com
www.klostergardentautra.no
Klostergården is a farm, bed and breakfast, restaurant, brewery and distillery. They produce whisky which is sold through their restaurant.

RUSSIA

PRASKOVEYA
ul. Lenin 11
s. Praskoveya The Budennovskiy region Stavropol territory 356817
Russia
Tel: (86559) 5-27-41
Email: info@praskoveya.ru
www.praskoveya.ru
Besides vodka and brandy they also produce Praskoveyskoe Whiskey which is distilled from malted barley and aged for three years in oak barrels.

SPAIN

DESTILERIAS LIBER SL
Poligono Industrial la Paloma Calle Mulhacen
18640 Padul Grenada
Spain
Tel: +34 958 796061
Email: info@destileriasliber.com
www.destileriasliber.com
They produce Vodka, Rum, and three types of whisky. Whisky Embrujo Granada is made from malted barley and aged in used American oak and Xerez wine barrels; Barrel Embrujo Whisky takes the same new spirit and matures it in a four liter barrel which shortens the time needed for aging and intensifies the oak flavors. Garafe Pure Malta is their un-aged malt spirit sold in two liter bottles.

DESTILERIAS Y CRIANZA DEL WHISKY SA
Camino Molino del Arco
40194 Palazuelos de Eresma
Segovia
Spain
Tel: +34 921 449 250
DYC offers two expressions of its peated whisky aged in American Oak — a 3-year and an 8-year.

SWEDEN

BACKAFALLSBYN AB
Norreborgsvägen 55
260 13 Sankt Ibb
Sweden
Tel: +46 (0) 418 449 999
Email: info@backafallsbyn.se
www.hven.com
In 2008 they began production of what they claim is Sweden's first Single Malt Whisky called Urania. It is pot distilled, aged for three years and bottled, unfiltered at cask strength.

BERGSLAGENS DESTILLERI AB
Pettersbergsvägen 2A
703 69 Örebro
Sweden
Tel: +46 (0) 708 235 682
Email: Built into their website
www.bergslagensdestilleri.se
In the summer of 2011 they began production of a new make spirit to be aged into a single malt whisky. Currently they are selling Scottish blended and single malt whiskies under their Engelbrekt Whisky lable. Interested parties can also buy their whisky by the cask which will age for three years before bottling.

BOX DESTILLERI
Box Kraftverk 140
87296 Bjartra
Sweden
Tel: +46 (0) 70 552 78 28
Email: info@boxdestilleri.se s
www.boxdestillerie.se
Dubbed as the world's northernmost distillery, Box Distillery plans to produce a Swedish single malt whisky using Scottish methods.

GAMMELSTILLA WHISKY AB
Gammelstillavägen 103 B
813 94 Torsåker
Sweden
Tel: +46 (0) 70 604 29 34
Email: info@gammelstilla.se
www.gammelstilla.se
Their distillery is just starting up and is experimenting with different grain bills which will be aged for three years into whisky.

GOTLAND DISTILLERY
Sockerbruket
622 54 Romakloster
Sweden
Tel: +46 (0) 498 27 29 00
Email: info@gotlandwhisky.se
www.gotlandwhisky.se
Founded in 2004 they are producing a peaty single malt whisky called Isle of Lime. The name come from the limestone base of the island on which they grow their own organic barley, harvest native peat and collect water. They also have plans to introduce other types of whisky in the future.

GRYTHYTTAN WHISKY
Ekeberg
S-705 98 Lillkyrka
Sweden
Tel: +46 (0) 73 73 123 68
Email: info@grythyttanwhisky.com
www.grythyttanwhisky.com
Though still in the beginning stages of production, Grythyttan Distillery plans to produce three expressions of its whisky, all with increasing intensity: a light floral, fruity whisky; a slightly smokier one; and a fuller, very smoky whisky; all matured in either ex-bourbon barrels or ex-sherry butts. Spirit production began in October 2010 and their first whisky should be ready near the end of 2013.

GUTE VINGÅRD
Hablingbo Hallbjäns
62342 Havdhem
Sweden
Tel: +46 498 48 70 70
Email: info@gutevin.se
www.gutevin.se
Operated by master distiller and blender Lauri Pappinen, they began production of what became their first whisky in 2004. Simply named Whisky Limited Edition 2013, it was matured in a pseudo-solera system that used a 225 liter Sherry cask, a 110 liter new Limousin barrel with a medium toast, and a 25 liter Hungarian cask that once held fortified wine and brandy. All the whisky started off in the Sherry cask and then some portion was moved to the other two barrels for a period of time. All of the 2013 whisky was bottled at 40% abv in 500ml bottles. The next release is still maturing.

LAPPLAND DESTILLERI
Järnvägsgatan 91
933 33 Arvidsjaur
Sweden
Email: info@lapplanddestilleri.se
lapplanddestilleri.se
Under construction. No production yet.

MACKMYRA SVENSK WHISKY AB
Bruksgatan 4
818 32 Valbo
Sweden
Tel: +46 8 556 025 80
Email: info@mackmyra.se
www.mackmyra.se

Hailed as the first whisky distillery in Sweden, Mackmyra offers an extensive range of smoked and un-smoked malts, aged in various casks, such as Sherry, bourbon, and Swedish oak. Their Special series matures their whisky in 30 and 100 liter barrels each of which is finished in casks that once held fruit wines or coffee. Their Moment series is bottled from individual barrels that display a unique personality. They also sell their whisky in small barrels.

NORRTELJE BRÄNNERI
Lohärad PL 104 77
761 72 Norrtälje
Sweden
Tel: +46 176 22 71 30
Email: info@norrteljebrenneri.se
www.norrteljebrenneri.se

Promoted as Sweden's first organic whiskey, Roslagswhisky Eko no. 1 was distilled in 2009 and has been maturing in 30 liter Sherry casks. It a silver medal at the 2012 Destillata spirit competition in Austria. Pre-orders of individual bottles sold out before its 2014 release but whole casks were still available for sale as of June 2013.

SMÖGEN WHISKEY AB
Ståleröd Ljungliden 1
Hunnebostrand, Sverige
Sweden
Tel: +46 (0) 76 162 63 03
Email: Built into their website
www.smogenwhisky.se

Their intentions are to only produce for the Swedish and (possibly) Scandinavian market. The distillery is a simple pot still operation which seeks to produce a distinctly west coast Scandinavian whisky, taking inspiration from the Scottish west coast. Their malt is thus peaty and the spirit character fairly intense. Distilling started in August, 2010 and is aging in European Oak, as well as ex-Bourbon and sherry casks for three years before bottling.

SPIRIT OF HVEN DISTILLERY
Backafallsbyn AB
Norreborgsvagen 55
260 13 Sankt Ibb
Sweden
Tel: +46 (0) 418 449 999
Email: info@hven.com
www.hven.com

Spirit of Hven is an organic certified craft distillery in southern Sweden. In 2008 they began production of what they claim is Sweden's first Single Malt Whisky called Urania. It is made from local barley that is malted and kilned at their distillery. It is then pot distilled, aged for three years and bottled, unfiltered at cask strength. They have recently released Hven Dubhe Single Malt Whisky which was matured in American, French and Spanish oak before being bottled unfiltered at 45% abv. Dubhe is the first of a seven part series released annually, each named after a star in the Big Dipper.

TEVSJÖ DESTILLERI
Tevsjövägen 1
820 40 Järvsö
Sweden
Tel: +46 (0) 70 72 72 174, +46 (0) 70 24 68 578
Email: tevsjodestilleri@gmail.com
www.tevsjodestilleri.se

Along with vodka, gin and a few other products they have begun the process of producing the first Swedish "Bourbon." While not technically bourbon for a variety of reasons, the grain bill consist of 52% corn, 48% barley. The spirit will be aged new barrels and used bourbon barrels for about 5 years and finished on aquavit barrels.

WANNBORGA BRÄNNERI & VINGÅRD
Övra Vannborga By 11
38796 Köpingsvik
Sweden
Tel: +46 (0) 485 829 13, +46 (0) 708 28 08 31, +46 (0) 708 28 29 28
Email: oingrid@wannborga.nu
www.wannborga.nu

They produce two single malt whiskies. Both were distilled in 2007 and matured in ex-Bourbon and ex-Sherry casks. Some of the whisky was bottled in 2011, after 4½ years, at 44% abv in 50cl bottles. Another portion of the whisky was bottled in 2012, after 5½ years, at 43.4% abv in 50cl bottles. Their Wannborga Whisky 5 years won a Bronze medal at the 2013 Destillata spirit competition in Austria.

SWITZERLAND

AKTIENBRAUEREI FLIMS SURSELVA AG
7018 Flims Waldhaus
Switzerland
Tel. +41 81 928 14 00
Email: info@surselva-bier.ch
www.surselva-bier.ch
This brewery and distillery produces two whiskies and two spirits made from beer. Their Flimser Whisky is a Swiss Single Malt Whisky that has been aged in oak barrels for at least three years, and their Reserve du Patron is a very rare whisky matured in small barrels. They also produce Surselva Bockbier, which is an unaged spirit made from winter bock beer and Urselva Lady Bierlikör is a liqueur made from a dark beer and an unaged grain spirit. While the latter two fall outside the legal definition of whisky in Europe they are similar to products being made by American craft distillers.

BRAUEREI AARE BIER
Neuenburgstr. 42
3282 Bargen BE
Switzerland
Tel 032 391 00 22
Email: info@aarebier.ch
http://www.aarebier.ch
This brewery and distillery produces three varieties of their Old River Midland Single Malt Whisky and one liqueur. The whisky is made from sustainable and locally grown barley and aged for four years in Swiss oak for their Classic bottling and in Amarone oak barrels for their Premium and Superior bottlings.

BRENNEREI ERISMANN
Dorfstrasse 6 Eschenmosen
8180 Bülach
Switzerland
Tel: +41 044 860 53 02
Email: info@brennerei-erismann.ch
www.brennerei-erismann.ch
This distillery produces a wide range of spirits, including: grappa, brandy, and absinthe. They have also produced one bottling of Zürcher Lowland Whisky which was made from malted barley and matured in a new American oak and ex-Bourbon barrels.

BRENNEREI HOLLE
Hollen 52
4426 Lauwil
Switzerland
Tel: +41 61 941 15 41
Email: m-hess@tiscalinet.ch
www.single-malt.ch
Founded in 1999, they were the first distillery to begin the process of making whisky the very same day Swiss law legalized its production. Hof Holle produces a number of whiskies aged in used French wine barrels for at least three years.

BRENNEREI KRAMER
Niederdorf 7
3412 Heimiswil
Switzerland
Tel: +41 034 422 73 19
Email: kontakt@brennerei-kramer.ch
www.brennerei-kramer.ch
This brandy distillery also produces two whiskies called Emmentaler Single Malt Whisky. One is bottled at 58% abv and the second at 43% abv.

BRENNEREI LÜTHY
Urs Lüthy
Suhr Gasse 27
5037 Muhen
Switzerland
Tel: +41 062 723 11 69
Email: info@brennerei-luethy.ch
www.brennerei-luethy.ch
They make a number of single malt whiskies from 100% Swiss Barley that they malt by hand and mature in an oak barrels for three years and one day. They are also producing Seetaler Urdinkel Spelt Whisky in partnership with Mühle Seengen. This whisky is made from 100% spelt and aged for three years in used Pinot Noir barrels.

BRENNEREI SCHWAB
Barweg 8
3298 Oberwil Bei Büren
Switzerland
Email: Built into their website
www.brennereischwab.ch
This distillery started producing whisky once the Swiss prohibition against whisky production ended in 1999. They make Bucheggberger Whisky which is aged for 5 years and bottled directly from the casks. They source their wort from Gasthausbrauerei Burgdorf. They are also distilling Tram Single Malt Whisky for Altes Tramdepot in Bern which is aged for three to six years in ex-wine barrels.

BRENNEREI STADELMANN
Unterdorf 5
6147 Altbüron
Switzerland
Tel: +41 062 927 20 17
Email: Built into their website
www.schnapsbrennen.ch

They produce five products from distilled malted barley. Dorfbachwasser and Dorfbachwasser Jubiläumsabfüllung malt whiskies were produced for the Melchnauer Whisky Club; Luzerner Hinterländer Single Malt they describe as a brandy because it has only been aged one year in oak barrels; Luzerner Hinterländer Single Malt Whisky Nr. 3 was aged three years in ex-cider barrels; Luzerner Hinterländer Single Malt Whiskey Nr. 4 was aged three years in merlot barrels.

BURGDORFER GASTHAUSBRAUEREI
Wynigenstrasse 13
Postfach 1085 - 3401 Burgdorf
Switzerland
Tel. +41 34 423 13 64
Email: info@burgdorferbier.ch
www.burgdorferbier.ch

This brewery and distillery produces 5 and 10-year old Burgdorfer Single Malt Whiskies which are only available for shareholders.

DISTILLERIE BRAUEREI LOCHER AG
Brauereiplatz 1
9050 Appenzell
Switzerland
Tel. +41 71 788 01 40
Email: mail@saentismalt.ch
www.saentismalt.ch

They produce four "Editions" of Säntis Malt Swiss Highlander Whisky and Säntis Cream Liqueur. They have also distilled whiskies for Hopfentropfen brewery in Unterstammheim and the Terreni alla maggia farm in Ascona.

DESTILLERIE HAGEN
Verena und Ueli Hagen Rühli
Seehof
8536 Huttwilen
Switzerland
Tel: +41 052 747 11 91
Email: info@distillerie-hagen.ch
www.distillerie-hagen.ch

Hagen's Best Swiss Single Malt Whisky is distilled three times and then matured in ex-bourbon barrels.

ETTER DISTILLERIE
Chollerstrasse 4
6300 Zug
Switzerland
Tel: +41 41 748 51 51
Email: etter@etter-distillerie.ch
http://www.johnett.ch
or http://www.etter-distillerie.ch

This long time fruit distillery founded in 1870 is now selling Johnett Swiss Single Malt Whisky. Their first release was produced in 2007 and aged for at least three years. They currently source their whisky wash from the Baar Brewery and mature their whisky in used Swiss oak wine barrels. Their whisky is proofed down with water from the near by Höllgrotten cave

GEBR. KÜMIN WEINBAU & WEINHANDEL AG
Oechsli 1
8807 Freienbach
Switzerland
Tel: +41 055 417 40 20
Email: info@kuemin-weine.ch
http://www.kuemin-weine.ch

This winery re-opened their distillery in 1998 and produces a variety of fruit spirits as well as two versions of their whisky. They make Two Ravens Single Malt Whisky which is matured in used Swiss wine barrels for three years and bottled at 43% abv. Their second offering is Two Ravens Single Malt Whisky San Gottardo which spends one of its tree years maturing in a cold and moist cavern and bottled at 45.5% abv.

HUMBEL SPEZIALITÄTENBRENNEREI
Baumgartenstrasse 12
5608 Stetten
Switzerland
Tel: +41 56 496 50 60
Email: humbel@humbel-brand.ch
www.humbel-brand.ch

A producer of a wide variety of spirits, they partner with Unser Bier to produce Our Beer Single Malt Whisky, which is aged for three years and bottled at 43% abv and a few bottles at 66% abv. The whisky is usually finished in Tokay barrels (a type of Hungarian wine) but some of the whisky is finished in sherry casks or whisky casks from Bowmore.

LANGATUN DISTILLERY AG
St. Urbanstrasse 34
4900 Langenthal
Switzerland
Tel: +41 79 336 00 17
Email: spirit@langatun.ch
www.langatun.ch
This distillery produces a range of spirits including Old Deer Single Malt Whisky and Old Bear Single Malt Smoked Whisky, both of which come in 40% abv and cask strength as well as Gold Bee Whisky Liqueur. They age their new make barley spirit in Swiss oak wine barrels for at least three years.

MACARDO GMBH
Strohwilen-Frauenfelderstrasse
8514 Amlikon-Bissegg
Switzerland
Tel: +41 079 679 87 77
Email: m.frauchiger@macardo.ch
www.macardo.ch
The primary products from the Macardo distillery are their Macardo Swiss Single Malt Whisky, which uses both barley and spelt; and Macardo Swiss Bourbon which uses corn, rye, malted barley and is aged in new charred American oak barrels.

MAISON LES VIGNETTES
Les Vignettes 6
1957 Ardon, Valais,
Switzerland
Tel: + 41 027 306 20 83
Email: swhisky@bluewin.ch
www.swhisky.ch
They produce three lines of Glen Vignettes Single Malt Whisky including the Collection Prestige line, which begins with the very light, fruity "Annouim" and ends with the powerful and peppery "Keugant."

MOSTEREI KOBELT
Staatsstrasse 21
9437 Marbach
Switzerland
Tel: +41 71 777 12 20
Email: info@mostereikobelt.ch
http://www.mostereikobelt.ch
They produce Glen Rhine Corn & Barley Whisky which is aged for three years and bottled at 40% abv.

RUGENBRÄU AG
Wagnerenstrasse 40
3800 Matten
Switzerland
Tel: +41 033 826 46 46
Email: Built into their website
www.rugenbraeu.ch
This brewery began producing whisky in 2010. They offer four bottlings of their Swiss Highland Single Malt Whisky, which before 2010 was distilled by Spezialitätenbrennerei Zürcher. Their whisky bottlings include: Classic; Forty Three; Ice Label, which is finished for one year in an ice cave, 3454m above sea level; and Century, also finished in their ice cave celebrates the 100th anniversary of the Jungfrau Railway. All of their whiskies are matured in 500 liters ex-Oloroso-Sherry butts for a minimum of three years.

SCHAUBRENNI Z'GRAGGEN
Seestrasse 56
6424 Lauerz
Switzerland
Tel. +41 811 55 22
Email: info@zgraggen.ch
www.schaubrennerei.ch
They produce Z'GRAGGEN three and an eight year old single malt whiskies. They also distill LiWHInthSKY, made from 30% corn and 70% malted barley for the Rappi Bier Factory.

SONNENBRÄU AG
Alte Landstrasse 36 Postfach 144
9445 Rebstein
Switzerland
Tel. +41 071 775 81 11
Email: info@sonnenbraeu.ch
www.sonnenbraeu.ch
The brewery also makes two types of Whisky. Their Ribel SwisslanderWhisky is made from corn grown in the Rhine Valley and malted barley. It had a limited edition release in 2005 after aging for four years but the remainder stayed in the barrels till 2011 and released as a 10-year old whisky. They have also begun production of Rheintaler Single Sunlander Malt Whisky which is made from all malted barley and aged like the Ribel Whisky in Spanish Sherry and Port casks as well as American, French and German Oak barrels.

SPEZIALITÄTENBRENNEREI ZÜRCHER
Nägeligässli 7
2562 Port
Switzerland
Tel: + 41 032 331 5 83
Email: info@lakeland-whisky.ch
www.lakeland-whisky.ch
This distillery produces Single Lakeland Malt Whisky, which is mature for at least three years in oloroso sherry casks. And up until 2010 they distilled whisky for Rugenbräu.

WHISKY CASTLE
Käsers Schloss AG
Schlosstrasse 17
5077 Elfingen
Switzerland
Tel: +41 62 876 17 83
Email: info@kaesers-schloss.ch
www.whisky-castle.com
Whisky Castle produces several different whiskies made from barley, rye, spelt, matured zin ex-bourbon, ex-sherry, ex-Scotch and Hungarian oak. They also produce Wädenswiler Single Malt Whisky for Wädi Brau Huus which supplies its own wort.

WHISKYVISION MONSTEINE AG
Hauptstrasse 15
7278 Davos Monstein
Switzerland
Tel: +41 079 461 68 89
Email: info@whiskyvision-monstein.ch
http://www.whiskyvision-monstein.ch
They produce a number of different bottlings under their Monsteiner Single Malt Whisky label. They are maturing their whiskies for about seven years before bottling at 40% abv.

Bushmills | Ireland

Bushmills Currently owned by Diageo, Ireland's oldest working distillery, which opened in 1608, produces two blended whiskies: White and Black; and three single malts whiskies: 10, 16 and 21 year old. [page 51]

ENGLAND | IRELAND | WALES

St. George's Distillery | England

St. George's Distillery They are the first English malt whisky distillery in over a decade to produce a range of malt spirits. They release the whiskies as a "Chapter" series. Matured 3 years, each chapter has been finished in different barrel types, like rum or sherry casks and they alternate between peated and un-peated malt. [page 51]

ENGLAND

CORNISH SCRUMPY CO. LTD
Truro
Cornwall TR4 9LW
United Kingdom
Tel: +44 01872 573356
Email: info@thecornishcyderfarm.co.uk
http://www.thecornishcyderfarm.co.uk/prodbrandy.htm
http://www.staustellbrewery.co.uk/whiskey

Also know as Healey's Cornish Cyder Farm, they collaborated with St. Austell Brewery to produce Hicks and Healey Cornish Single Malt Whisky. They whisky is made with Maris Otter barley grown in South Eastern Cornwall and local spring water. Their new make barley spirit is matured in once used Bourbon barrels for seven years before being bottled.

COPPER HOUSE DISTILLERY
East Green Southwold
Suffolk IP18 6JW
United Kingdom
Tel: +44 01502 727 225
Email: distillerytours@adnams.co.uk
www.adnams.co.uk/spirits/the-copper-house-distillery

Established in 2010, they are currently aging their spirit into whisky for future release as well as producing Gin and Vodka.

ST. GEORGE'S DISTILLERY
English Whisky Co, Ltd.
Harling Rd.
Roudham Norfolk NR16 2QW
United Kingdom
Tel: +44 01953 717939
Email: info@englishwhisky.co.uk
www.englishwhisky.co.uk/

They are the first English malt whisky distillery in over a decade to produce a range of malt spirits. They release the whiskies as a "Chapter" series. Matured 3 years, each chapter has been finished in different barrel types, like rum or sherry casks and they alternate between peated and un-peated malt.

IRELAND

BUSHMILLS
2 Distillery Rd., Bushmills
County Antrim
Northern Ireland
B757 8XH
Tel: +44 (0) 28207 33218
Email: visitors.bushmills@diageo.com
www.bushmills.com

Currently owned by Diageo, Ireland's oldest working distillery, which opened in 1608, produces two blended whiskies: White and Black; and three single malts whiskies: 10, 16 and 21-year old.

COOLEY DISTILLERY
Head Office:
162 Clontarf Rd.
Dublin 3
Tel: +353 (0)1 833 2833
Distillery:
Riverstown, Cooley
County Louth
Ireland
Tel: +353 (0) 42 937 6102
Email: info@cooleywhiskey.com
www.cooleywhiskey.com

Cooley produces a number of quality brands, including the peated Connemara, Greenore 8 Year Old Single Grain (distilled from corn), and Tyrconnell Single Malt Irish Whiskey. Beam Global currently owns them.

KILBEGGAN DISTILLERY
Bridge St.
Kilbeggan
Westmeath
Ireland
Tel: +353 (0)1 833 2833
Email: info@kilbegganwhiskey.com
www.kilbegganwhiskey.com

Founded in 1757, and currently owned by Cooley Distillery, a subsidiary of Beam Global. Kilbeggan is a blend of grain and malt whiskey and aged in ex-bourbon barrels. In 2007 they released a limited edition 15-year old whiskey.

MIDLETON
Midleton
County Cork
Ireland
Tel: +353 1850 774 748
Email: info@idl.ie
www.irishdistillers.ie

Opperated by Irish Distillery, a subsidiary of Pernod Ricard, Midleton distillery produces a number of triple distilled Irish whiskies including Jameson and Tullamore Dew.

Penderyn Distillery| Wales

PENDERYN After a 100 year absence of distilleries in Wales, Penderyn came on the scene in recent years with its light Penderyn Single Malt. [page 53]

THE DINGLE WHISKEY DISTILLERY
Dingle
Kerry
Ireland
Tel: +353 66 915 0699
Email: distilled@dingledistillery.ie
www.dingledistillery.ie

The Dingle distillery is the westernmost distillery in Europe on the southwest coast of Ireland. Dingle is producing single malt spirit that will age in former Bourbon, Port, Sherry and a variety of ex-wine casks. Currently their first 500 whiskey barrels are being sold individually as part of their Founding Fathers program that carries with it certain benefits. Barrel 501 and on will be aged for about 5 years before the various single malt casks are blended and bottled.

WALES

PENDERYN DISTILLERY
The Welsh Whisky Company
Penderyn Distillery
Penderyn
Wales
CF44 0SX
Tel: +44 01685 813 300
Email: Built into their website
www.welsh-whisky.co.uk

After a 100 year absence of distilleries in Wales, Penderyn came on the scene in recent years and is producing four expressions of its single malt: Madeira Finished, Sherrywood, and Peated Single Malt Whisky as well as Penderyn's Single Cask Whisky. They are currently owned by Sazerac.

SCOTLAND

Springbank | Scotland

The Springbank distillery makes several brands and expressions, such as Springbank 10-year Old Single Malt Whisky, the heavily peated Longrow 10-year Campbeltown Single Malt Whisky, and the 8-year Old Hazelburn Triple Distilled Campbeltown Single Malt Whisky. A 12-year old version of Hazelburn was also released in 2009. [page 57]

CAMPBELTOWN

GLEN SCOTIA
12 High St.
Campbeltown
Argyll PA28 6DS
Scotland
Tel: +44 1586 552288
Email: glenscotia@btconnect.com
www.glenscotia-distillery.co.uk

Glen Scotia produces a 12 and 14-year old single malt whisky as well as a variety of cask strength single, peated and heavily peated malt whiskies.

MITCHELL'S GLENGYLE DISTILLERY CO LTD
85 Longrow
Campbeltown
Argyll PA28 6EX
Scotland
Tel: +44 (0)1586 552009
Email: info@kilkerran.com
www.kilkerran.com

Kilkerran Single Malt Whisky is due to be released as a 10-year old in 2014 and a 12-year in 2016 although visitors can currently sample younger versions in the distillery tasting room.

SPRINGBANK
85 Longrow
Campbeltown
Argyll PA28 6EX
Scotland
Tel: +44 (0)1586 552009
Email: Built into their website
www.springbankdistillers.com

The Springbank distillery makes several brands and expressions, such as Springbank 10-year Old Single Malt Whisky, the heavily peated Longrow 10-year Campbeltown Single Malt Whisky, and the 8-year Old Hazelburn Triple Distilled Campbeltown Single Malt Whisky. A 12-year old version of Hazelburn was also released in 2009.

HIGHLANDS

ABERFELDY DISTILLERY
Aberfeldy
Perthshire PH15 2EB
Scotland
Tel: +44 (0)1887 822010
Email: worldofwhisky@dewars.com
www.dewarswow.com

Currently owned by Bacardi Ltd., the Aberfeldy distillery was founded by John Dewer & Sons. Currently they produce the Aberfeldy 12-Year Old and 21-Year Old Single Malt whiskies.

ADELPHI DISTILLERY LTD
Glenborrodale Castle
Ardnamurchan
Argyll PH36 4JP
Scotland
Tel: +44 (0) 1972 500765
Email: Built into their website
www.adelphidistillery.com

Originally founded in 1826, this distillery closed its doors in 1907 and was revived as an independent bottler in 1993. Currently under construction, the new Adelphi Distillery is expected to be completed and producing single malt spirit by the end of 2013.

ARDMORE
Kennethmont
Huntly
Aberdeenshire AB54 4NH,
Scotland
Tel: +44 (0)1 1464 831213

Currently owned by Beam Global, the Ardmore distillery produces malts that are mostly used in blended whiskies. Ardmore also produces some rich, smoky whiskies such as the Ardmore 12-year old Single Malt.

BALBLAIR DISTILLERY
Edderton
Tain
Ross-shire IV19 1LB
Scotland
Tel: +44 (0)1862 821273
Email: Built into their website
www.balblair.com

Balblair offers a number of vintage whiskies, including the '65, '75, '78, '89, '96 and 2001. Currently they are owned by Inver House Distillers.

BEN NEVIS DISTILLERY
Lochy Bridge
Fort William
Highland PH33 6TJ
Scotland
Tel: +44 (0)1397 702476
Email: colin@bennevisdistillery.com
www.bennevisdistillery.com

The Ben Nevis distillery puts out a large range of expressions, such as the 10, 12, 14-Year Old Single Sherry Cask, 15, and 30-year old, and a 1990 Port Wood Finish Single Malt.

Balblair | Scotland

Balblair Balblair offers a number of vintage whiskies, including the '65, '75, '78, '89, '96 and 2001. Currently they are owned by Inver House Distillers. [page 57]

BLAIR ATHOL
Perth Rd.
Pitlochry
Perthshire PH16 5LY
Scotland
Tel: +44 (0)1796 482003
Email: blair.athol.distillery@diageo.com
www.discovering-distilleries.com/blairathol
Founded in 1826 and currently owned by Diageo, this distillery produces Blair Athol 12-Year Old Single Malt Whisky.

CLYNELISH DISTILLERY
Brora
Sutherland
Highland KW9 6LR
Scotland
Tel: +44 (0)1408 623000
Email: clynelish.distillery@diageo.com
www.discovering-distilleries.com/clynelish
Owned by Diageo, Clynlish Brora makes 14 year old Coastal Highlands Single Malt, a 15-year old Distillers Edition, plus Distillery Only edition bottled at 57.3% abv.

DALMORE DISTILLERY
Alness
Rosshire
Highland IV17 0UT
Scotland
Tel: +44 (0)1349 882362
Email: Built into their website
www.thedalmore.com
Founded in 1839 they produce The Dalmore 12, 15, and 18-Year Old expressions as well as the Grand Reserve, King Alexander III, and Astrum.

DALWHINNIE DISTILLERY
Dalwhinnie
Inverness-shire
Highland PH19 1AB
Scotland
Tel: +44 (0)1540 672219
Email: dalwhinnie.distillery@diageo.com
www.discovering-distilleries.com/dalwhinnie
Founed in 1897 and currently owned by Diageo, Dalwhinnie offers a 15-Year Old and 18-Year Old Distillers Edition.

DEANSTON DISTILLERY
Doune
Perthshire FK16 6AG
Stirling
Scotland
Tel: +44 (0)1786 841422
Email: deanstonmalt.com/contact/
www.burnstewartdistillers.com
Founded in 1966 and currently owned by Burn Stewart Distillers Ltd, this eastern Highlands distillery produces a un-chillfiltered cask strength single malt whisky.

EDRADOUR DISTILLERY
Pitlochry
Perthshire PH16 5JP
Scotland
Tel: +44 (0)1796 472095
www.edradour.com
Edradour, Scotland's smallest distillery produces a 10-year old, and a cask strength single malt whisky.

FETTERCAIRN
Distillery Rd.
Fettercairn
Laurencekirk AB30 1YB
Scotland
Tel: +44 (0)01561 340205
www.fettercairndistillery.co.uk
Currently owned by Whyte and Mackay, Fettercairn bottles Fior, which is a blend of a number of their different vintages as well as a 24, 30 and 40-Year Old Scotch Malt Whisky

GLENCADAM
Brechin
Angus DD9 7PA
Scotland
Tel: +44 (0)1356 622217
Email: dfitchett@glencadamdistillery.co.uk
www.glencadamdistillery.co.uk
Glencadam distillery produces five single malt whiskies includes a 10, 12, 14, 15 and 21-year old expression. They also produce whisky that Angus Dundee uses for blending.

GLENDRONACH
Forgue, By Huntly
Aberdeenshire AB54 6DB
Scotland
Tel: +44 (0)1466 730202
Email: info@glendronachdistillery.co.uk
www.glendronachdistillery.co.uk
Founded in 1826, GlenDronach produces six single malt whiskies ranging in age from 12 to 33 years old. They also produce four single malts that have each been finished in Tawny Port, Moscatel, Virgin Oak, or Sauternes.

GLEN GARIOCH
Distillery Rd.
Oldmeldrum
Aberdeenshire AB51 0ES
Scotland
Tel: +44 (0)1651 873450
Email: Built into their website
www.glengarioch.com
Glen Garioch's produces a 12-year old and a Founders Reserve Single Malt Whisky. They also from time to time bottle a limited single cask series from their stock of maturing whisky.

GLENGLASSAUGH
Portsoy
Aberdeenshire AB45 2SQ
Scotland
Tel: +44 (0)1261 842367
Email: info@glenglassaugh.com
www.glenglassaugh.com
Over 100 years old when it closed down in 1986, Glenglassaugh was resurrected in 2008. While they wait for their some of their whisky to age they are bottling 26, 30 and 41-year old casks that were made before the distillery shut down in '86. They are also selling some of their new make spirit for use in cocktails or on its own.

GLENGOYNE DISTILLERY
Dumgoyne
Sterling G63 9LB
Scotland
Tel: +44(0)1360 550254
Email: reception@glengoyne.com
www.glengoyne.com
The Glengoyne Distillery produces a very wide range of whiskies that vary in age from 8 years to over 30. Some of their whiskies are made from unpeated malt, some are unchill filtered and most are bottled at cask strength.

GLENMORANGIE
Tain
Ross-shire IV19 1BR
Scotland
Tel: +44 (0)1862 892477
Email: website@glenmorangie.co.uk
www.glenmorangie.com
In 2007, Glenmorangie relaunched its portfolio of whiskies. The Original 10-year old Single Malt Whisky serves as the base for all their other products. They produce an "Extra Matured" series that takes the 10-year old and ages them in French wine, Port, or Sherry casks for an additional two years. They also make a "Private Edition" series as well as three older bottlings one of which included chocolate malt in the grain bill.

GLEN ORD
Muir of Ord
Ross-shire IV6 7UJ
Highland
Scotland
Tel: +44 (0)1463 872004
Email: glen.ord.distillery@diageo.com
www.discovering-distilleries.com/glenord
Currently owned by Diageo, Glen Ord produces a 12-year old single malt Scotch called "The Singleton of Glen Ord" which is only for sale in Asia and at the visitor center.

GLENTURRET
The Hosh
Crieff
Perth and Kinross PH7 4HA
Scotland
Tel: +44 (0)1764 656565
Email: Built into their website
www.thefamousgrouse.com
Currently owned by the Edrington Group, The Glenturret distillery produces whisky that goes into The Famous Grouse Scotch Whisky.

LOCH EWE
Drumchork Estate
Aultbea IV22 2HU
Scotland
Tel: +44 (0)1445 731242
Email: info@lochewedistillery.co.uk
www.lochewedistillery.co.uk
The Loch Ewe micro-distillery produces "illicit style," or new make whisky, such as its Spirit of Loch Ewe and Uisge Single Malt.

LOCH LOMOND
Lomond Estate
Alexandria G83 0TL
Scotland
Tel: +44 (0)1389 752781
Email: mail@lochlomonddistillery.com
www.lochlomonddistillery.com
Loch Lomond's range includes Loch Lomond Single Malt, a 21-year old, and Loch Lomond Single Blend Whisky, which is a blend of their malt and grain whiskies.

OBAN
Stafford St.
Oban
Argyll & Bute PA34 5NH
Scotland
Tel: +44 (0)1631 572004
Email: Oban.distillery@diageo.com
www.discovering-distilleries.com/oban
Currently owned by Diageo, This urban distillery makes a 14-year old and Distillers Edition expression of its whisky.

OLD PULTENEY
Huddart St.
Wick
Highland KW1 5BA
Scotland
Tel: +44 (0)1955 602371
Email: Built into their website
www.oldpulteney.com
Founded in 1826, Old Pulteney's produces a 12, 17, 21, and 30-year old whisky. The 17 and 21-year old spend extra time to finish in Sherry casks. Currently they are owned by Inver House Distillers.

ROYAL BRACKLA
Cawdor
Nairn
Highland, IV12 5QY
Scotland
Tel: +44 (0)1667 402002
Currently owned by Bacardi Ltd., Royal Brackla distillery makes a 10-year old and limited edition 25-year old single malt.

ROYAL LOCHNAGAR
Balmoral
Crathie
Ballater
Aberdeenshire AB35 5TB
Scotland
Tel: +44 (0)1339 742700
Email: Royal.Lochnagar.Distillery@diageo.com
www.discovering-distilleries.com/royallochnagar
Currently owned by Diageo, Royal Lochnagar produces a 12-year old, a Select Reserve without an age statement and a Distillers Edition.

TEANINICH
Alness
Highland IV17 0XB
Scotland
Tel: +44 (0)1349 885001
Founded in 1817 and currently owned by Diageo, the Teaninich distillery rarely produces single malts because most of the production is used in other blended whiskies.

TULLIBARDINE
Sterling St.
Blackford
Perthshire PH4 1QG
Scotland
Tel: +44 (0)1764 682252
Email: Built into their website
www.tullibardine.com
Tullibardine's produces single malt whiskies; one finished in Sherry casks, another in Banyuls(fortified wine) casks. They also produce a few vintage and single cask bottlings.

WOLFBURN
Henderson Park,
Thurso
Caithness KW14 7XW
Scotland
Email: info@wolfburn.com
www.wolfburn.com
This new distillery began producing single malt spirits in 2013. They are maturing the spirit in a variety of woods including ex-Bourbon barrels and former Spanish sherry butts. 2016 is the earliest their product can be sold as single malt whisky but it is likely the will choose to age it a bit longer.

ISLANDS

ABHAINN DEARG
Carnish
Isle of Lewis
Outer Hebrides HS2 9EX
Scotland
Tel: +44 (0)1851 672429
Email: Built into their website
www.abhainndearg.co.uk
Abhainn Dearg holds the distinction of being the first legal whisky distillery on the Outer Hebridean Isle of Lewis since at least 1840, and it is also the westernmost distillery in Scotland. The distillery also produces its own barley. In 2010 they bottled their first Single Malt whisky and they also sell the Spirit of Lewis which is younger than 3 years because it is not labeled whisky.

ARRAN
Shore Rd.
Lochranza
Isle of Arran
North Ayrshire, KA27 8HJ
Scotland
Tel: +44 (0)1770 830334
Email: Built into their website
www.arranwhisky.com
The sole distillery on the Isle of Arran, they produce a wide range of whiskies. Most notably, Arran

Ardbeg | Islay

Ardbeg Established in 1815, and most recently reopened in 1997, Ardbeg produces: a 10 year old, that is un-chill filtered and bottled at 46%; the heavily peated Supernova; the Corryvreckan; the Uigeadail finished in sherry casks; and the lightly peated Blasda. Currently the French company LVMH Moët Hennessy Louis Vuitton owns the distillery. [page 63]

distillery produces a standard 10-year old, 14-year old and two Single Cask whiskies in bourbon and sherry wood. They also produce a line of whiskies finished in Amarone, Sauternes, and Port casks which they release as part of their Cask Finnish Program.

HIGHLAND PARK
Holm Rd.
Kirkwall
Orkney KW15 1SU
Scotland
Tel: +44 (0)1856 874619
Email: Built into their website
www.highlandpark.co.uk
Currently owned by the Edrington Group, Highland Park is Scotland's northern-most distillery on the Isle of Orkney. They produces a range of whiskies, including 12, 15, 18, 25, 30, and 40-years old. They also produce four series of rare, special and limited addition bottlings.

ISLE OF JURA DISTILLERY
Craighouse
Isle of Jura
Argyl, PA60 7XT
Scotland
Tel: +44 (0)1496 820240
Email: info@isleofjura.com
www.isleofjura.com
The range of whiskies produced by Isle of Jura Distillery includes: a 10, and 16-year old; the Superstition which is lightly peated; the Prophecy which is heavily peated; and a series of limited edition bottlings.

SCAPA
St. Ola
Kirkwall
Orkney KW15 1SE
Scotland
Tel: +44 (0)1856 872071
Email: info@scapamalt.com
www.scapamalt.com
Scapa distillery currently produces a 16-Year Old Single Malt Whisky.

TALISKER DISTILLERY
Carbost
Isle of Skye, IV47 8SR
Scotland
Tel: +44 (0)1478 614308
Email: talisker@diageo.com
www.discovering-distilleries.com/talisker
This distillery, the only one on the Isle of Skye, produces several expressions of its whisky, including a 10, 18, 25-year, as well as a Distiller's Edition. Currently they are owned by Diageo.

TOBERMORY
Main St.
Tobermory
Isle of Mull
Argyllshire PA75 6NR
Scotland
Tel: +44 (0)1688 302647
Email: Built into their website
www.tobermorymalt.com
Currently owned by Burn Stewart Distillers, Ltd., Tobermory is the only legal distillery on the Isle of Mull and produces whisky under the Tobermory and Ledaig labels. Tobermory is an unpeated malt whisky that comes in a 10 and 15-year bottling, while Ledaig, is a peated version, bottled as a 10-year old single malt whisky.

ISLAY

ARDBEG DISTILLERY
Port Ellen
Isle of Islay
Argyll PA42 7EA
Scotland
Tel: +44(0)1496 302244
Email: Built into their website
www.ardbeg.com
Established in 1815, and most recently reopened in 1997, Ardbeg produces: a 10 year old, that is un-chill filtered and bottled at 46%; the heavily peated Supernova; the Corryvreckan; the Uigeadail finished in sherry casks; and the lightly peated Blasda. Currently the French company LVMH Moët Hennessy Louis Vuitton owns the distillery.

BOWMORE
School St.
Bowmore
Isle of Islay
Argyll PA43 7JS
Scotland
Tel: +44 (0)1496 810441
Email: info@morrisonbowmore.co.uk
www.bowmore.co.uk
This Islay distillery produces a variety of whiskies, starting with the standard Bowmor, 12, 15, 18, and 25-year old single malt whisky. They also produce a Limited Edition series and a special 40-year old bottling. Bowmore is currently owned by a subsidiary of Suntory.

Laphroaig | Scotland

Laphroaig One of the peatiest Scotch whiskies comes in a range of 10, 18, and 25-year old single malts as well Cask Strength, Quarter Cask, Triple Wood and PX Cask. [page 65]

BRUICHLADDICH
Rhinns Peninsular
Isle of Islay
Argyll PA49 7UN
Scotland
Tel: +44 (0)1496 850221
Email: Built into their website
www.bruichladdich.com
Established in 1881, Bruichladdich offers four different series of un-peated Scotch Whisky: Classic, Provenance, Concept and Rare. They also produce two series of peated Scotch Whisky: Port Charlotte and Octomore, which seems to have the goal of being the most heavily peated Scotch. Currently the French company Rémy Cointreau owns this distillery.

BUNNAHABHAIN
Shore Rd.
Bunnahabhain
Isle of Islay
Argyll PA46 7RP
Scotland
Tel: +44 (0)1495 840646
Email: Built into their website
www.bunnahabhain.com
Bunnahabhain Distillery produces 12, 18, and 25-year old lightly peated whiskies. Currently Burn Stewart Distilleries Ltd. owns them.

CAOL ILA DISTILLERY
Port Askaig
Isle of Islay
Argyll PA46 7RL
Scotland
Tel: +44 (0)1496 302760
Email: caolila.distillery@diageo.com
www.discovering-distilleries.com/caolila
Caol Ila's core expressions are the 12 and 18-year old, as well as a Cask Strength and Distiller's Edition. Currently they are owned by Diageo.

KILCHOMAN
Rockside Farm
Bruichladdich
Isle of Islay
Argyll PA49 7UT
Scotland
Tel: +44 (0)1496 850011
Email: info@kilchomandistillery.com
www.kilchomandistillery.com
Established in 2005, Kilchoman is a farm distillery that grows and floor malts its own barley. They mature their whisky in Bourbon barrels from Buffalo Trace and Sherry casks from Spain. They currently produce a 3-year old Single Malt Whisky and 100% Islay From Barley to Bottle Whisky. They are the only private distillery remaining in Islay.

LAGAVULIN
Port Ellen
Isle of Islay
Argyll PA42 7DZ
Scotland
Tel: +44 (0)1496 302250
Email: lagavulin.distillery@diageo.com
www.discovering-distilleries.com/lagavulin
Lagavulin produces 12, and 16-year old single malts and a special Distiller's Edition. They are open for tours and are close to two other Islay Distilleries. Currently they are owned by Diageo.

LAPHROAIG
Port Ellen
Isle of Islay
Argyll, PA42 7DU
Scotland
Tel: +44 (0)1496 302418
Email: info@laphroaig.com
www.laphroaig.com
Currently owned by Beam Global. Laphroaig is known for consistently producing some the peatiest Scotch whiskies. Their seven variations include: 10-year old Single Islay Malt, bottled at 40% abv and Cask Strength; 18 and 25-year old bottlings; Quarter Cask, which is partially aged in smaller oak barrels to increase the maturation process; as well as Triple Wood and PX Cask which finishes the Quarter Cask in Oloroso or Pedro Ximenez sherry casks.

LOWLANDS

AILSA BAY SCOTCH WHISKY DISTILLERY
Girvan
Ayrshire, KA26 9PT
Scotland
Tel: +44 (0)1465 713091
Owned by William Grant & Sons, they began operation in 2007. Most of their distillate will be used in the Grants blended whisky and currently they do not offer a single malt.

ANNANDALE DISTILLERY COMPANY LTD
Annan
Dumfriesshire, DG12 5LL
Scotland
Email: d.thomson@annandaledistillery.com
www.annandaledistillery.co.uk
Closed in 1919, Annandale is under new owner as of 2007 and is currently restoring and rebuilding the distillery. They are hoping to begin production as soon as possible and produce a smoky single

malt whisky. They are also hoping to open a whisky academy.

AUCHENTOSHAN
Old Kilpatrick
Dalmuir, Duntocher,
Dunbartonshire, G81 4SG
Scotland
Tel: +44 (0)1389 878561
Email: info@morrisonbowmore.co.uk
www.auchentoshan.co.uk
Auchentoshan currently distills six expressions of its whisky: the Classic, 12, 18, 21-years, and Three Wood (in American bourbon, oloroso and Pedro Ximinez sherry casks), as well as a Limited Edition series.

BLADNOCH DISTILLERY
Bladnoch
Dumfries and Galloway DG8 9AB
Scotland
Tel: +44 (0)1988 402235
Email: Raymond@bladnoch.co.uk
www.bladnoch.co.uk
Bladnoch distillery offers its whisky either as a whole cask or bottled. Bottled editions include an 8, 9 10, 19 and 20-year old Single Malt as well as a Distillers Choice.

CAMERONBRIDGE DISTILLERY
Leven Windygates
Fife KY8 5R
Scotland
Tel : +44 (0)1343 547433
Currently owned by Diageo, they produce grain whisky and have an annual capacity upwards of 100,000,000 liters.

DAFTMILL
By Cupar
Fife KY15 5RF
Scotland
Tel: +44 (0)1337 830303
Email: info@daftmill.com
www.daftmill.com
The new Daftmill micro-distillery grows and malts its own barley, and is currently aging its whisky in bond.

GIRVAN
Grangestone industrial Estate Girvan
South Ayrshire KA26 9PT
Scotland
Currently owned by William Grant & Sons, they produce grain whisky with a annual capacity of 15,000,000 liters some of which is bottled as Black Barrel Single Grain Whisky.

GLENKINCHIE
Pencaitland, Tranent
East Lothian, EH34 5ET
Scotland
Tel: +44 (0)1875 342004
Email: malts.com@consumer-care.net
www.malts.com
This Lowland distillery currently makes Glenkinchie 12-year old and Distiller's Edition finished in amontillado sherry casks. Diageo currently owns them.

KINGSBARNS COMPANY OF DISTILLERS LTD
Kingsbarns St.Andrews
Fife, KY16 8QD
Scotland
Tel: +44 (0)7717 754053
Email: doug@kingsbarnsdistillery.com
www.kingsbarnsdistillery.com
Near St. Andrew golf course, Kingsbarns will produce a cask strength single malt whisky made partially from on-site floor malted barley and matured exclusively in 100 liter "quarter casks."

NORTH BRITISH DISTILLERY
9 Wheatfield Rd.
Edinburgh, EH11 2PX
Scotland
Tel: +44 (0)1313 373363
Email: info@northbritish.co.uk
www.northbritish.co.uk
Partially owned by Diageo and Edrington Group they produce grain whisky and have an annual capacity upwards of 64,000,000 liters. They sell their whisky for blending in The Famous Grouse, J&B Rare, Johnnie Walker Black Label, and Cutty Sark.

STRATHCLYDE DISTILLERY
40, Moffat St.
Glasgow G5 0
Scotland
Tel: +44 (0)1414 292024
Founded in 1927 and currently owned by Pernod Ricard, Strathclyde produces about 40 million liters of grain whisky per year.

SPEYSIDE

ABERLOUR
High St.
Banffshire, AB38 9PJ
Scotland
Tel: +44 (0)1340 881249
Email: aberlour.admin@pernod-ricard.com
www.aberlour.com
The Aberlour distillery's core range consists of a 10, 12, 16, 18-year old and the un-chill filtered A'bunadh which was finished in Sherry casks and bottle at cask strength.

ALLT-A-BHAINNE
Glenrinnes
Dufftown
Banffshire AB55 4DI
Scotland
Tel: +44 (0)1340 20837
Email: information@pernod-ricard.fr
Founded in 1975 this distillery supplies malt for blended whiskies like Chivas Regal and is currently owned by Pernod Ricard.

AUCHROISK
Mulben
Keithe, AB55 6XS
Scotland
Tel: +44 (0)1542 885000
Founed in 1974 by Diageo, Auchroisk single core product is the Auchroisk 10-year Single Malt. They also produce whisky for J&B.

AULTMORE
Keith
Banffshire, AB55 6QY
Scotland
Tel: +44 (0)1542 881800
Currently owned by Bacardi Ltd., Aultmore produces the Aultmore 12-Year Old Single Malt Whisky though most of the distillery's production goes into the Dewer's blend.

BALMENACH
Cromdale
Moray, PH26 3PF
Scotland
Tel: +44 (0)1479 872569
Email: enquiries@inverhouse.com
www.inverhouse.com/distilleries-balmenach.php
Currently owned by Inver House Distillers, Balmenach is aging its whisky until they think it's ready for bottling.

BALVENIE
Dufftown
Keith
Banffshire, AB55 4DH
Scotland
Tel: +44 (0)1340 820373
Email: Built into their website
www.thebalvenie.com
The Balvenie produces seven core bottlings and two limited edition bottlings including DoubleWood, aged 12 years, Single Barrel, aged 15 years, and PortWood, aged 21 years. Currently the distillery is owned by William Grant & Sons.

BENRIACH
Elgin
Morayshire, IV30 8SJ
Scotland
Tel: +44 (0)1343 862888
Email: info@benriachdistillery.co.uk
www.benriachdistillery.co.uk
Located in the "Heart of the Speyside" the BenRiach distillery was built in 1898 and it produces a very wide range of single malt whiskies. Their classic range includes a bottling with no age statement as well as a 12, 16, and 20-year old bottling. Their other five ranges include a peated and special wood finish bottlings.

BENRINNES
Aberlour
Banffshire, AB38 9NN
Scotland
Tel: +44 (0)1340 872600
Email: malts.com@consumer-care.net
www.malts.com
First established in 1826 and currently owned by Diageo, Benrinnes produces most of its whisky for blends such as J&B, it also produces a 15-year single malt.

BENROMACH
Invererne Rd.
Forres
Moreyshire, IV36 3F.B
Scotland
Tel: +44 (0)1309 675968
Email: info@benromach.com
www.benromach.com
Owned and managed by Gordon & MacPhail, the Benromach distillery offers a few different series of single malt bottlings. They have a standard range that includes a 10, 21, 25, and 30-year old single malt whiskies. They also produce organic, cask strength, peated, wood finish and vintage series.

BRAEVAL
Chapeltown
Banffshire, AB37 9JS
Scotland
Tel: +44 (0)1542 783042
Currently owned by Pernod Ricard, the Braeval Distillery mostly produces whisky for blending. Some of its whisky has been bottled as Deerstalker Highland Single Malt.

CARDHU
Knockando
Aberlour
Banffshire, AB38 7RY
Scotland
Tel: +44 (0)1340 872555
Email: cardhu.distillery@diageo.com
www.discovering-distilleries.com/cardhu
Currently owned by Diageo, Cardhu's primary releases are a 12-Year Old Single Malt Whisky and a Special Cask Reserve.

CRAGGANMORE
Ballandalloch
Banffshire, AB37 9AB
Scotland
Tel: +44 (0)1479 874635
Email: cragganmore.distillery@diageo.com
www.discovering-distilleries.com/cragganmore
Currently owned by Diageo, Cragganmore produces a 12 and 21-Year Old Single Malt Whisky as well as a Distillers Edition.

CRAIGELLACHIE
Craigellachie
Aberlour
Banffshire, AB38 9ST
Tel: +44 (0)1340 872971
Currently owned by Bacardi Ltd., about 2% of their whisky is bottled as a 14-Year Single Malt Scotch Whisky, while the rest is used in Dewer's white label blend.

DAILUAINE
Carron
Banffshire, AB38 7RE
Tel: +44 (0)1340 872500
Email: malts.com@consumer-care.net
www.malts.com
Currently owned by Diageo, this distillery's core whisky is a 16-year old single malt, although it has also released a 17-year old Manager's Dram aged in sherry casks.

DUFFTOWN
Dufftown
Keith
Banffshire, AB55 4BR
Tel: +44 (0)1340 822100 / 820224
Originally opened in 1896, Diageo currently owns the Dufftown Distillery and produces the 12-year old Singleton of Dufftown as its core product sold in the European market.

GLENALLANCHIE
Aberlour
Banffshire, AB38 9LR
Scotland
Tel: +44 (0)1542 783042/ 871315 / 871204
One of Scotland's youngest distilleries, Glenallanchie opened in 1967 and is currently owned by Pernod Ricard. The vast majority of their production goes into a variety of blended whiskies like Clan Campbell but in 2005 they releases a 16 year old Cask Strength Single Malt Whisky aged in oloroso sherry casks.

GLENBURGIE
Forres
Morayshire, IV36 2QY
Scotland
Tel: +44 (0)1343 850258
Pernod Ricard currently owns the Glenburgie distillery and uses the majority of the production in Ballantine's and Old Smuggler blended whiskies. The last official bottling was a 15-year old single malt scotch released in 2002.

GLENDRONACH
Forgue
Aberdeenshire
Speyside, AB54 6DB
Scotland
Tel: +44 (0)1466 730202
Email: info@glendronachdistillery.co.uk
www.glendronachdistillery.com
Founded in 1826 and reopened in 2008 by the BenRiach Distillery Company, GlenDronach produces 12, 15, 18, 21, 31, and 33-year old single malt whiskies. They also produce a series of bottlings with four different wood finishes and a wide variety of single cask bottleings.

GLENDULLAN
Dufftown
Keith
Banffshire, AB55 4DJ
Scotland
Tel: +44 (0)1340 822100
Founded in 1898 and currently owned by Diageo, their core release is a 12-year old Singleton of Glendullan which is sold in the US market.

GLEN ELGIN
Longmore
Morayshire, IV30 3SL
Scotland
Tel: +44 (0)1343 862100
Currently owned by Diageo, Glen Elgin produces a 12 and 16-year old version of their single malt whisky.

GLENFARCLAS
Ballindalloch
Banffshire, AB37 9BD
Scotland
Tel: +44 (0)1807 500257
Email: info@glenfarclas.co.uk
www.glenfarclas.co.uk
Glenfarclas is a family owned distillery that produces a wide range of single malt whiskies, including a 10, 12, 15, 17, 21, 25, 30, and 40-year old single malt whisky as well as a variety of cask strength, reserve and single cask bottlings.

GLENFIDDICH
Dufftown
Keith
Banffshire, AB55 4DH
Scotland
Tel: +44 (0)1340 820373
Email: info@glenfiddich.com
www.glenfiddich.com
Currently owned by William Grant & Sons, Glenfiddich produces a large range of whiskies. The core collection includes their flagship 12-year old single malt and four other bottlings. They also produce a rare and vintage reserve line that includes older and limited batch bottling.

GLEN GRANT
Elgin Rd.
Rothes
Banffshire, AB38 7BS
Scotland
Tel: +44 (0)1340 832118
Email: visitorcentre@glengrant.com
www.glengrant.com
Founded in 1840 and currently owned by the Campari Group, Glen Grant's core expressions are a 5, 10 and 16-year old single malt Scotch, as well as two special edition bottlings.

GLENLIVET
Ballindalloch
Banffshire, AB37 9DB
Scotland
Tel: +44 (0)1340 821720
Email: theglenlivet.admin@pernod-ricard.com
www.theglenlivet.com
Founded in 1824 and currently owned by Pernod Ricard, Glenlivet produces a Classic Range that includes five aged single malts from 12 to 25 years old; the Nadurra line represents three un-chill filtered single malts; the Cellar Collection represents a wide assortment of vintage whiskies from their considerable stock.

GLENLOSSIE
Birnie
Elgin
Morayshire, IV30 3SS
Scotland
Tel: +44 (0)1343 862000
Founded in 1876 and currently owned by Diageo, Glenlossie uses most of its production for blended whiskies. About 0.5% of their production goes towards making a 10 year old single malt.

GLEN MORAY
Bruceland Rd.
Elgin
Morayshire, IV3 1YE
Scotland
Tel: +44 (0)1343 550900
Email: Built into their website
www.glenmoray.com
This brewery-turned-distillery has a wide range of whiskies which consists of a Classic (no age statement), 12, 16, and 30-year old, and several vintage malts, such as 1962, 1964, 1991, and 1995. The French company La Martiniquaise currently owns Glen Moray.

GLENROTHES
Physical Address:
Rothes
Morayshire, AB38 7AA
Scotland
Postal Address:
BB&R Spirits Ltd
3 St James's St.
London SW1A 1EG
Tel: +44 (0)1340 872300
Email: contactus@bbrspirits.com
www.theglenrothes.com
Founded in 1879, this distillery produces one standard bottling called The Glenrothes Select Reserve, and a wide selection of vintage bottlings from 1975 to 1998.

GLEN SPEY
Rothes
Morayshire, AB38 7AU
Scotland
Tel: +44 (0)1340 831215
Founded in 1878 and currently owned by Diageo, most of Glen Spey's whisky goes into blends, particularly J&B but it also produces a rare 12-year old single malt.

GLENTAUCHERS
Mulben
Keith
Banffshire, AB55 6YL
Scotland
Tel: +44 (0)1542 860272
Currently owned by Pernod Ricard, the vast majority of their production goes into blended whiskies but several independent bottlings from this distillery exists, such as Glentauchers 1990 by Gordon & MacPhail.

HUNTLY DISTILLERY
Huntly
Aberdeenshire, AB54
Scotland
Tel: +44 (0)1466 794055
Email: info@duncantaylor.com
www.duncantaylor.com
Duncan Taylor is a bottling company that is in the planning phases to build Scotland's first carbon neutral distillery. They want to begin production of their own Single Malt and Single Grain Whiskies.

INCHGOWER
Buckie
Banffshire, AB56 5AB
Scotland
Tel: +44 (0)1542 836700
Currently owned by Diageo, about 99% of Inchgower's production goes into blended whiskies like Bells and White Horse. The remaining 1% goes into an official bottling of a 14-year old single malt.

KININVIE DISTILLERY
Dufftown
Keith
Banffshire, AB55 4DH
Scotland
Email: info@wgrantusa.com
www.grantusa.com/index.php?q=locations/distilleries
Owned by William Grant & Sons, they built the Kininvie Distillery behind the Balvine Distillery and mostly produces whisky for blending. Some of the whisky has been released under the name Hazelwood, or the brand Monkey Shoulders aimed at younger non-Scotch drinkers.

KNOCKANDO
Knockando
Morayshire, AB38 7RT
Scotland
Tel: +44 (0)1340 882000
Email: malts.com@consumer-care.net
www.malts.com/index.php/en_us/Our-Whiskies/Knockando
Currently owned by Diageo, Knockando produces a 12, 18, and 21-year old single malt whisky.

KNOCKDHU
Knock, by Huntly
Aberdeenshire, AB54 7LJ
Tel: +44 (0)1466 771223
Email: Built into their website
www.ancnoc.com
The Knockdhu distillery's core product is anCnoc 12-year old Highland Single Malt Scotch Whisky. They also produce a 16-year old un-chill filtered single malt and several vintage bottlings. Currently they are owned by Inver House Distillers.

LINKWOOD
Elgin
Morayshire, IV30 3 RD
Tel: +44 (0)1343 862000
Currently owned by Diageo, the Linkwood distillery produces most of its whisky for use in the Johnnie Walker and White Horse blends but it has also bottled a 12-year old single malt.

LONGMORN
Longmore
Morayshire, IV30 3SJ
Scotland
Tel: +44 (0)1343 554139
Email: information@pernod-ricard.fr
Currently owned by Pernod Ricard, Longmorn's main whisky is a 16-year old expression

MACALLAN
Easter Elchies
Craigellachie
Morayshire, AB38 9RX
Scotland
Tel: +44 (0)1340 871471
Email: Built into their website
www.themacallan.com
Currently owned by the Edrington Group, Macallan's large range consists of several core lines, such as the classic Sherry Oak, Fine Oak, Fine and Rare, and Vintage. Expressions from these lines include the Macallan 18-year old Sherry Oak, Macallan 17-year old Fine Oak, and the Macallan 1926, 60 years old.

MACDUFF
Banff
Aberdeenshire, AB45, UK
Scotland
Tel: +44 (0)1261 812612
Owned by Bacardi, the MacDuff Distillery produces Glen Deveron 12-year old Single Malt Scotch Whisky.

MILTONDUFF
Elgin
Morayshire, IV30 8TQ
Scotland
Tel: +44 (0)1343 547433
Email: information@pernod-ricard.fr
Currently owned by Pernod Ricard, Miltonduff produces most of its whisky for Ballantine's blended whisky. Some of its production is used in a 10-year old single malt.

MANNOCHMORE
Elgin
Morayshire, IV30 8SS
Tel: +44 (0)1343 862000
Currently owned by Diageo, Mannochmore's primary whisky is Mannochmore 12-year old.

MORTLACH
Dufftown
Keith
Banffshire, AB55 4AQ
Scotland
Tel: +44 (0)1340 822100
Owned by Diageo, the Mortlach production contributes to Johnnie Walker Black Label blend as well as Mortlach 16-year old single malt whisky.

ROSEISLE DISTILLERY
Roseisle
Moray IV30 5YP
Scotland
Tel: +44 (0)1343 832100
Opened in 2010 by Diageo to increase production for their Johnny Walker and Buchanan's whiskies. Roseisle is trying to achieve carbon neutral production with an attached £14m biomass plant.

SPEYBURN
Rothes
Aberlour
Moreyshire, AB38 7AG
Scotland
Tel: +44 (0)1340 831213
Email: Built into their website
www.speyburn.com
Founded in 1897, the Speyburn distillery produces and bottles three different expressions: The Bradan Orach (no age statement) as well as a 10-year Old and 25-year old Highland Single Malt Scotch Whisky. Currently they are owned by Inver House Distillers.

SPEYSIDE
Glen Tromie
Kingussie
Inverness-Shire, PH21 1NS
Tel: +44 (0)1540 661060
Email: info@speysidedistillers.co.uk
www.speysidedistillery.co.uk
Founded in 1990, this small distillery produces The Speyside 12-year Single Highland Malt, a 5-year Drumguish Single Highland Malt, and a variety other blended Scotch whiskies.

STRATHISLA
Seafield Ave.
Keith
Banffshire, AB55 5BS
Scotland
Tel: +44 (0)1542 783044
Email: strathisla.admin@pernod-ricard.com
www.maltwhiskydistilleries.com
Currently owned by Pernod Ricard, Strathisla produces Strathisla 12-year old single malt whisky and 15-year old Cask Strength. Much of their production also goes towards use in Chivas Regal Blended Scotch Whisky.

STRATHMILL
Keith
Banffshire, AB55 3DQ
Scotland
Tel: +44 (0)1542 883000
Founded in 1891 and currently owned by Diageo, Strathmill produces whisky for use in blends and for a 12-year old single malt.

TAMDHU
Knockando
Aberlour
Morayshire, AB38 7RP
Tel: +44 (0)1340 872200
Most of Tamdhu's production was used in blended whiskies. In 2011 they were sold to Ian MacLeod. Production is suppose to resume under the new ownership but it is uncertain when.

TAMNAVULIN
Tomnavulin
Ballindalloch
Banffshire, AB3 9JA
Scotland
Tel: +44 (0)1807 590285
Tamnuvulin's current expression is a 12-year old, although it has released a 22, 25 and 29-year olds in

the past. In 2007 it was sold to Indian businessman Vijay Mallya and production has resumed.

TOMATIN
Tomatin
Inverness-shire, IV13 7YT
Scotland
Tel: +44 (0)1808 511444
Email: info@tomatin.co.uk
www.tomatin.com
Tomatin's range consists of Tomatin 12, 18, 25, 30, and 40-year old whiskies, 1970 Cask Bottling, and Antiquary 12 and 21-year old whiskies.

TOMINTOUL
Ballindalloch
Banffshire, AB37 9AQ
Scotland
Tel: +44 (0)1807 590274
Email: rfleming@tomintouldistillery.co.uk
www.tomintouldistillery.co.uk
Dubbed as "the gentle dram," Tomintouls's range of whiskies encompasses the Tomintoul 10, 14, 16 and 27-year old single malt whiskies, a 12-year old malt finished in Oloroso Casks, and a 1976 Vintage among others.

TORMORE
Tomre Advie
Grantown-on-Spey
Morayshire, PH26 3LR
Scotland
Tel: +44 (0)1807 510244
Currently owned by Pernod Ricard, Tormore's whisky contributes to Long John blended whisky as well as a 12-year old single malt whisky.

Pemberton | British Columbia

Pemberton Pemberton Valley Single Malt Whisky is currently maturing in ex-Bourbon barrels and will be bottled in three to five years. The whisky is produced from 100% organic malted barley from Armstrong BC. [page 77]

CANADA

66 GILEAD DISTILLERY
66 Gilead Rd.
Bloomfield, Ontario K0K 1G0
Tel: (613) 393-1890
Email: info@66gileaddistillery.com
www.66gileaddistillery.com

While 2012 marked their first year of production, they are already selling their vodka and gin and began producing a couple of Canadian rye spirits. One expression will be a 100% pot distilled Rye Whisky aged for at least three years in Canadian oak. While Canada requires a spirit to be aged at least 3 years before it can be called whisky, 66 Gilead plans to mature their spirit as long as it needs to attain the character they are looking for.

ALBERTA DISTILLERS (AKA CARRINGTON DISTILLERS LTD)
1521 34 Ave. SE
Calgary, Alberta T2G 1V9
Canada
Tel: (403) 265 2541
Email: tsimpson@jbbworld.com

Founded in 1946, Alberta Distillers is currently owned by Beam Global and its products include Alberta Premium 5-year old and Alberta Springs 10-year old whiskey.

CANADIAN MIST
Georgian Bay
Collingwood, Ontario
Canada
Email: Built into their website
www.canadianmist.com

Now a subsidiary of Brown-Forman, the Canadian Mist distillery produces Canadian Mist whisky.

GIMLI
Distillery Rd.
Gimli, Manitoba R0C 1B0
Canada
Tel: (204) 642 5123
Email: CrownRoyal@consumer-care.net
www.crownroyal.com

Currently owned by Diageo, the Gimli distillery makes several rye whiskies, such as Crown Royal and Crown Royal XR.

GLENORA DISTILLERY
Physical Address:
13727 Ceilidh Trail, Route 19,
Glenville, Nova Scotia B0E 1X0
Canada
Postal Address:
PO Box 181,
Mabou, Nova Scotia B0E 1X0
Canada
Tel: 1 800 839 0491
Email: info@glenora1.ca
www.glenoradistillery.com

Glenora is the maker of Glen Breton Rare Canadian Single Malt Whisky which is double distilled in two large copper pot stills.

HIGHWOOD
114-10th Ave. S.E.
Box 5893
High River, Alberta T1V 1M7
Canada
Tel: (403) 652 3202
Email: hrplant@telus.net
www.highwood-distillers.com

The Highwood Distillery expressions include Centennial 10-Year Old Canadian Rye Whisky, 15-Year Plus Century Reserve Canadian Rye Whisky, and Century Reserve 21-Year Old Canadian Rye Whisky.

HIRAM WALKER & SONS
Canadian Club Brand Heritage Center
2072 Riverside Dr. East
Windsor, Ontario N8Y 4S5
Canada
Tel: (519) 973 9503
Email: Built into their website
www.canadianclubwhisky.com

Partially owned by both Beam Global and Pernod Ricard, The Hiram Walker & Sons Distillery's expressions include Canadian Club whiskies, Walker Special Old and Wisers Canadian whiskies.

KITTLING RIDGE WINERY & DISTILLERY
297 South Service Rd.
Grimsby, Ontario L3M 1Y6
Canada
Tel: 1 800 694 6798
Email: jhall@kittlingridge.com
www.kittlingridge.com

The Kittling Ridge Winery & Distillery's whiskies include Forty Creek Barrel Select, Forty Creek Double Barrel Reserve, and Mountain Rock Canadian Whisky. They are currently owned by Sazerac.

LB DISTILLERS
1925 Avenue B North
Saskatoon, SK S7T 1B6
Tel: (306) 979 7280
Email: lucky@luckybastard.ca
www.luckybastard.ca

Lucky Bastard is working on two Canadian whiskies. They make their Single Malt Canadian Whisky from 100% Munich malted barley grown and malted in the Canadian prairies. It is fermented and distilled on the grain and is barreled in once used Wild Turkey Bourbon barrels for 3, 5, and 10 years then finished in French oak for the last 6 months. They also produce a Single Malt Rye Whisky, made with 75% malted rye and 25% Munich malted barley both grown and malted in Canada. Their Rye whisky will also be fermented and distilled on the grain, and aged for 3 years in once used Wild Turkey Bourbon barrels.

MYRIAD VIEW ARTISAN DISTILLERY INC
1336 Route 2
Rollo Bay, Prince Edward Island C0A 2B0
Canada
Tel: (902) 687 1281
Email: info@straitshine.com
www.straitshine.com

They produce Strait Whisky, which is made from a variety of grains and aged fore at least 3 years in American Oak.

OKANAGAN SPIRITS
First Address:
2920 28th Ave,
Vernon, British Columbia V1T 1V9
Canada
Tel: (250) 549 3120
Second Address:
267 Bernard Ave.
Kelowna, British Columbia V1Y 6N2
Canada
Tel: (778) 484 5174
Email: info@okanaganspirits.com
www.okanaganspirits.com

They produce Okanagan Spirits Whisky which is a blend of Canadian Rye Whisky from outside distilleries and Okanagan Spirit which is proofed down and bottled. They are currently working on a Single Malt Whisky made entirely of malt from British Columbia.

PALLISER
2925 9th Ave. N
Lethbridge, Alberta T1H 5E3
Canada
Tel: (403) 317 2128
www.cbrands.com/our-brands/spirits

Palliser Distillery makes Black Velvet Canadian Whisky and Black Velvet 8-year Reserve Canadian Whisky. They are currently owned by the wine producer Constellation Brands.

PEMBERTON DISTILLERY
Physical Address:
1954 Venture Place
Pemberton, British Columbia V0N 2L0
Canada
Postal Address:
PO Box 76
Pemberton, British Columbia V0N 2L0
Canada
Tel: (604) 894 0222
Email: info@pembertondistillery.ca
www.pembertondistillery.ca

Their Pemberton Valley Single Malt Whisky is currently maturing in ex-Bourbon barrels and will be bottled in three to five years. The whisky is produced from 100% organic malted barley from Armstrong BC.

SHELTER POINT DISTILLERY
4650 Regent Rd.
Campbell River, British Columbia V9H 1E3
Canada
Tel: (778) 420 2200
Email: info@shelterpointdistillery.com
www.shelterpointdistillery.com

Situate on Vancouver Island, they plan to release their Single Malt Whisky which was pot distilled and aged in used bourbon barrels in 2014.

STILL WATERS DISTILERY
50 Bradkwick Dr., Unit #26
Concord, Ontario L4K 4M7
Canada
Tel: (905) 482 2080
Email: info@stillwatersdistillery.com
www.stillwatersdistillery.com

Founded in 2009 they are currently maturing Single Malt, Rye, and Corn Whiskies that will be released as single cask limited editions in numbered bottles.

Victoria Spirits | British Columbia

Victoria Spirits is currently aging a spirit they will call Craigdarroch Whisky. The spirit was produced on a wood-fired copper pot still from 100% Canadian malted barley. It spent is first year in a 46L new American Oak barrel and will finish its maturation in used bourbon barrels. [page 79]

VALLEYFIELD DISTILLERY
(SCHENLEY DISTILLERIES)
1 Rue Salaberry Ouest
Salaberry-De-Valleyfield, Quebec Qc J6T 2G9
Tel: (450) 373 3230
Currently owned by Diageo, they are producing whisky for their Seagram's VO brand.

VICTORIA SPIRITS
6170 Old West Saanich Rd.
Victoria, British Columbia V9E 2G8
Canada
Tel: (250) 544 8217
Email: info@victoriaspirits.com
www.victoriaspirits.com
They are currently aging a spirit they will call Craigdarroch Whisky. The spirit was produced on a wood-fired copper pot still from 100% Canadian malted barley. It spent is first year in a 46L new American Oak barrel and will finish its maturation in used bourbon barrels.

Four Roses | United States

The Four Roses distillery produces several products, including Four Roses Small Batch Bourbon and Four Roses Single Barrel Bourbon. [page 83]

USA Whiskey Distilleries

Buffalo Trace | Kentucky

Buffalo Trace distillery makes Buffalo Trace Kentucky Straight Bourbon, George T. Stagg Kentucky Straight Bourbon, and Rock Hill Farm Single Cask Bourbon. [page 83]

INDIANA

LAWRENCEBURG DISTILLERS INDIANA
7 Ridge Ave.
Greendale, IN 47025
Tel: (812) 537 0700
Email: Built into their website
www.mgpingredients.com
Currently owned by MGP, they are a large scale producer of corn whiskey, 95% rye whiskey, 40% bourbon whiskey, (60% corn 40% other grains), 25% bourbon whiskey (75% corn 25% other grains), and corn bourbon whiskey.

KENTUCKY

BERNHEIM
1701 West Breckenridge
Louisville, KY 40210
Tel: (502) 585 9100
Email: Built into their website
www.heavenhill.com
The Bernheim distillery makes Bernheim Original Kentucky Straight Wheat Whiskey. Currently they are owned by Heaven Hill Distilleries.

BOULEVARD DISTILLERY
1525 TYRONE RD.
Lawrenceburg, KY 40342
1417 Versailles Rd.
Lawrenceburg, KY, 40342
Tel: (502) 839 4544
Email: wildturkey@qualitycustomercare.com
www.wildturkeybourbon.com
The Boulevard Distillery makes a range of Wild Turkey brand products, such as Wild Turkey Rare Breed and Wild Turkey Kentucky Straight Bourbon 8 years old. The Campari Group currently owns Wild Turkey.

BROWN-FORMAN
850 Dixie Hwy.,
Louisville, KY, 40210
Email: Brown-Forman@b-f.com
www.brown-forman.com
This facility distills and rectifies products for Brown-Forman's wide range of products.

BUFFALO TRACE
113 Great Buffalo Trace
Frankfort, KY 40601
Tel: (502) 696 5926
Sazerac Plan
2001 Highway 60 E.
Ownesboro, KY 42303
Tel: (502) 348-3991
Barton 1792 Plant
300 Barton Rd.
Bardstown, KY 40004
Tel: (502) 348-2991
Email: info@buffalotrace.com
www.buffalotrace.com
Owned by Sazerac, the Buffalo Trace distilleries makes Buffalo Trace Kentucky Straight Bourbon, George T. Stagg Kentucky Straight Bourbon, Rocky Hill Farm Single Cask Bourbon, Van Winkle Special Reserve, 1792 Ridgemont Reserve, Very Old Barton, Ten High and others.

EARLY TIMES DISTILLERY
2921 Dixie Highway
Louisville, KY 40216
Tel: 1 800 753 4567
Email: earlytimes@b-f.com
www.earlytimes.com
Founded in 1935, this Brown-Forman owned distillery makes Old Forester Kentucky Straight Bourbon.

FOUR ROSES
1224 Bond Mill Rd.
Lawrenceburg, KY 40432
Tel: (502) 839 3436
624 Lotus Rd. Hwy. 1604
Coxs Creek, KY 40013
Tel: (812) 537 0700
Email: info@fourroses.us
www.fourroses.us
Currently owned by the Kirin Brewery Co. the Four Roses distillery produces several products, including Four Roses Small Batch Bourbon and Four Roses Single Barrel Bourbon. They are currently producing the bourbon that goes into Bulleit Bourbon.

HEAVEN HILL
1701 W. Breckenridge St.
Louisville, KY 40210
1064 Loretto Rd,
Bardstown, KY, 40004
Tel: (502) 348 3921
Email: Built into their website
www.heavenhill.com
This family-owned distillery produces Elijah Craig Bourbon, Evan Williams Kentucky Bourbon and Rittenhouse Rye Whiskey.

Heaven Hill | Kentucky

Heaven Hill This family-owned distillery produces Elijah Craig Bourbon, Evan Williams Kentucky Bourbon and Rittenhouse Rye Whiskey. [page 83]

JIM BEAM
Visitor Center
149 Happy Hollow Rd.
Claremont, KY 40110;
Clermont Plant
526 Happy Hollow Rd.
Clermont, KY, 40110;
(502) 543-2221
Booker Noe Plant
1600 Lebanon Junction Rd.
Boston, KY 40197
(502) 833-4611
Frankfort Plant
Georgetown Rd.
Frankfort, KY 40601
(502) 695-3010
Email: Built into their website
www.jimbeam.com
Beam produces a wide range of bourbon brands, such as Baker's Kentucky Bourbon, Basil Hayden's Kentucky Bourbon, and Knob Creek Bourbon.

KENTUCKY BOURBON DISTILLERS
1869 Loretto Rd.
Bardstown, KY 40004
Tel: (502) 348 0081
Email: kentuckybourbon@bardstown.com
www.kentuckybourbonwhiskey.com
This distillery produces Noah's Mill Bourbon, Willett, and the Vintage Rye and Vintage Bourbon collections of whiskeys.

LABROT & GRAHAM (WOODFORD RESERVE)
7855 McCracken Pike
Versailles, KY 40383
Tel: (859) 879 1812
www.labrot-graham.com
This distillery makes Woodford Reserve Bourbon for the Brown-Forman company.

MAKER'S MARK
3350 Burks Spring Rd.
Loretto, KY 40037
Tel: (270) 865 2099 / 2881
Email: Built into their website
www.makersmark.com
The Maker's Mark distillery produces Maker's Mark Straight Bourbon. In 2010 they also began producing Maker's 46 which is aged longer with French Oak Staves. Currently they are owned by Beam Global.

TENNESSEE

CASCADE
1950 Cascade Hollow Rd.
Tullahoma, TN 37388
Tel: (931) 857 4110
Email: Built into their website
www.dickel.com
Currently owned by Diageo, the distillery produces George Dickel Cascade Hollow, George Dickel No. 8, George Dickel No. 12, and George Dickel Barrel Select Tennessee Whisky.

JACK DANIEL'S
182 Lynchburg Highway,
Lynchburg, TN 37352
Tel: (931) 759 4221
Email: info@jackdaniels.com
www.jackdaniels.com
Currently owned by Brown-Forman, the Jack Daniel's distillery produces Jack Daniel's Old No. 7, Gentleman Jack, and Jack Daniel's Single Barrel Tennessee Whiskey.

VIRGINIA

A. SMITH BOWMAN
1 Bowman Dr.,
Fredericksburg, VA 22408
Tel: (540) 373 4555
Email: Built into their website
www.asmithbowman.com
Owned by Sazerac, A. Smith Bowman produces Virginia Gentleman Straight Bourbon and Virginia Gentleman 90 Proof Small Batch Bourbon.

ROUGHSTOCK DISTILLERY | MONTANA

ROUGHSTOCK Products include Baby Blue Whisky, made from blue corn, as well as a peated and non-peated version of Balcones Single Malt Whisky. [page 101]

USA Craft Distilleries

ALASKA

ALASKA DISTILLERY
1540 North Shoreline Dr.
Wasilla, AK 99654
Tel: (907) 382-6250
Email: info@alaskadistillery.com
www.alaskadistillery.com
Along with Vodka, they produce Alaska Outlaw Whiskey, which is aged for three years in oak barrels. They say that it is a bourbon-style which indicates that their grain bill consists of 51% corn.

ARIZONA

ARIZONA DISTILLING CO
508 West First St.
Tempe, AZ 85281
Tel: (602) 391-3889
Email: info@azdistilling.com
www.azdistilling.com
They are just at the beginning stages of production, with the plan to offer four types of whiskey. At first they will offer a "White" whisky or New Make spirit while their other spirits are maturing in honeycomb barrels. Eventually they will offer an Arizona Bourbon, Rye Whiskey and an Arizona Whiskey made from locally grown Arizona durum wheat.

ARIZONA HIGH SPIRITS DISTILLERY
4366 East Huntington Dr., Suite B
Flagstaff, AZ 86004
Tel: (928) 853-1021
Email: info@arizonahighspirits.com
www.arizonahighspirits.com
Among other spirits they produce High Spirits Single Malt Mesquite Smoked Arizona Whisky. They use two-row barley and smoke it over locally harvested mesquite. There is no age statement.

HAMILTON DISTILLERS
209 North Hoff Ave.
Tucson, AZ 85705
Tel: (520)245-8471
Still under construction, they plan to produce whiskey in a copper pot still.

ARKANSAS

ROCK TOWN DISTILLERY
1216 East 6th St.,
Little Rock, AR 72202
Tel: (510) 907-5244
Email: info@rocktowndistillery.com
www.arkansaslightning.com
Rock Town Distillery is Arkansas' first "legal" distillery since prohibition, they make Arkansas Hickory Smoked Whiskey and Arkansas Young Bourbon Whiskey.

CALIFORNIA

1512 SPIRITS
State Farm Dr., Unit 11
Rohnert Park, CA 94928
Tel: (707) 843-9188
Email: info@1512spirits.com
www.1512spirits.com
Currently they make 1512 Barbershop Rye Whiskey, which is an unaged, 100% rye whiskey, 1512 Aged Rye Whisky and 1512 Spirits 2nd Chance Wheat Whiskey. They are also making a old Irish style moonshine called Poitin from 95% potato and 5% barley. All of their whiskies are double distilled before bottling.

AMERICAN CRAFT WHISKEY DISTILLERY
1110 Bel Arbres Rd. #D
Redwood Valley, CA 95470
Tel: (707) 468-4661
Email: ansley@craftdistillers.com
www.craftdistillers.com
Along with world class brandy and absinth this distillery produces Low Gap Whiskey by Crispin Cain. The whisky is made from 100% malted Bavarian hard wheat. In the next year or so they also plan to release Rye Whisky, an Oat Whiskey as well as a Corn Whiskey, approximately 80% yellow corn distilled with an admix of malted oat, barley, and rye.

ANCHOR DISTILLING COMPANY
1705 Mariposa St.
San Francisco, CA 94107
Tel: (415) 863-8350
Email: info@anchorsf.com
www.anchordistilling.com
Once owned by craft beer pioneer Fritz Maytag, Anchor Distilling produces three whiskies from 100% malted rye. Old Potrero Single Malt 18th Century Style Whiskey is aged in uncharred oak barrels for a minimum of 2.5 years; Old Potrero Single Malt 19th Century Style Straight Rye

Whiskey is aged in new charred oak barrels for over 4.5 years; and Old Potrero Hotalings Single Malt Whiskey, which bottles one barrel per year for release commemorating the 1906 San Francisco Earthquake and Fire, and celebrates the City's rebirth.

BALLAST POINT SPIRITS
10051 Old Grove Rd., Ste. B1
San Diego, CA 92131
Tel: (858) 695-2739
Email: yuseff@ballastpoint.com
www.ballastpoint.com

Along with Vodka, Gin, and Rum Ballast Point produces Devil's Share Whiskeys which are currently maturing before they are released. Devil's Share Single Malt Whiskey is made from 100% 2 row malted barley and will be maturing in a new heavy charred American oak for a minimum of three years. Devil's Share Bourbon is 61% corn, 30% 2 row barley and 9% malted wheat and will be maturing in a new heavy charred American oak for a minimum of three years.

BOWEN'S SPIRITS
1901 Mineral Court, Ste G
Bakersfield, CA 93308
Email: wade@bowenspirits.com
www.bowenspirits.com

They produce Bowen's Whiskey.

CHARBAY WINERY & DISTILLERY
4001 Spring Mountain Rd.
St. Helena, CA 94574
Tel: (707) 963-9327
Email: info@charbay.com
www.charbay.com

Known for its wide variety of high quality flavored vodkas, Charbay produces two whiskeys. Charbay Whiskey was produced from 20,000 gallons of Pilsner and a small quantity has been released in 2002 and 2008 at 3 years old and 9 years old. They also produce R5 Hop Flavored Whiskeys which were distilled from Bear Republic's Racer 5 IPA. R5 Aged was matured for 22 months in French oak while R5 Clear was aged one day in oak so it could be called whiskey. Both are bottled at 99 proof.

DRY DIGGINS DISTILLERY
5050 Robert J Mathews Pkwy., #100
El Dorado Hills, CA 95762
Email: info@drydiggings.com
www.drydiggings.com

While under construction they were planning to get their first new make spirits in the barrel by the end of 2012 Their initial plan is to produce two corn based whiskies and one rye based whiskey. Most of their grain will be sourced from local organic farmers as well as some grown on their own land.

The whiskeys will be aged in American oak barrels with a medium char in the foothills of California's Sierra Nevada mountains.

ESSENTIAL SPIRITS
144 A&B South Whisman Rd.
Mountain View, CA 94041
Tel: (650) 962-0546
Email: service@essentialspirits.com
www.essentialspirits.com

They produce Classick the Original American Bierschnaps, which is an un-aged spirit, distilled from a micro-brewed California Pale Ale. While they describe the spirit as a schnapps it is essentially un-aged malt spirit.

FOG'S END DISTILLERY
425 Alta St. Building 15
Gonzales, CA 93926
Tel: (831) 809-5941
Email: craig@fogsenddistillery.com
www.fogsenddistillery.com

They produce four different whiskies: Monterey Rye, California Moonshine, White Dog, and "Hand Craft Your Flavor" Whiskey which comes with an oak stave that can be added to the bottle and left in till the desired level of oak flavor is reached.

GREENBAR COLLECTIVE
2459 East 8th St.
Los Angeles, CA 90021
Tel: (213) 375-3668
Email: melkon@greenbar.biz
www.greenbar.biz

All the produce used by GreenBar is certified organic. They are currently working on Slow Hand white whiskey and eventually an aged whiskey.

OAKSTONE SPIRITS
Box 1089
Goleta, CA 93722
Tel: (805) 680-4009
Email: info@oakstonespirits.com
www.oakstonespirits.com

While still in the application phase this soon to be distillery anticipates making American style whiskeys based on corn, rye and wheat, aged in a range of barrel sizes and char levels for about 2 years.

OLD WORLD SPIRITS
121 Industrial Rd. #3-4
Belmont, CA 94002
Tel: (650) 424-1888
Email: info@oldworldspirits.com
www.oldworldspirits.com

Among a wide variety of spirits they produce Goldrun Rye California Whiskey. It is made from

100% un-malted Organic rye that is distilled like an Eau De Vie.

SPIRIT WORKS DISTILLERY
6790 McKinley St., #100
Sebastopol, CA 95472
707-731-9667
Email: hello@spiritworksdistillery.com
spiritworksdistillery.com

In Summer 2012 they begin batch distilling straight wheat whiskey and straight rye whiskey that will be aged in new, charred American white oak barrels for at least 2 years. They plan to be a complete "grain to glass" distillery that uses organic California-grown grain, which will be milled, mashed, fermented, distilled, aged, and bottle entirely at the distillery.

ST. GEORGE SPIRITS
2601 Monarch St.
Alameda, CA 94501
Tel: (510) 769 1601
Email: info@stgeorgespirits.com
www.stgeorgespirits.com

St. George produces St. George Single Malt Whiskey and they are also experimenting with producing a Bourbon. Their Breaking & Entering Bourbon is a blend 80 different barrels that they brought back from Kentucky.

ST. JAMES SPIRITS
5220 Fourth St., Unit 17
Irwindale, CA 91701
Tel: (626) 856 6930
Email: Sjspirits@earthlink.net
www.saintjamesspirits.com

This distillery makes Peregrine Rock California Pure Malt Whisky which is made from peated Highland Scottish Barley and aged in ex-Bourbon casks for two years.

STILLWATER SPIRITS
611 Second St.
Petaluma, CA 94952
Tel: (707) 778 6041
Email: stillwaterspirits@gmail.com
www.stillwaterspirits.com
www.moylandsdistilling.com

Stillwater Spirits produce Moylan's Bourbon Whiskey, Moylan's American Rye Whiskey and they are currently aging a whiskey that will be released as Moylan's Double Barrel Cask Strength Single-Malt Whiskey.

TAHOE MOONSHINE DISTILLERY
1611 Shop St. #4B
Box 551182
South Lake Tahoe, CA 96150
Tel: (530) 416-0313
Email: jeffrey@tahoemoonshine.com
www.tahoemoonshine.com

They produce Tahoe Moonshine Stormin' Whiskey, which is made from non-GMO young corn and aged in ex-Canadian whiskey barrels that have been planed and re-charred.

VALLEY SPIRITS
553 Mariposa Rd.
Modesto, CA 95354
Tel: (209) 484-0311
Email: masterdistiller@drinkvalleyspirits.com
www.drinkvalleyspirits.com

Besides vodka they also produce Moonshine Bandits Outlaw Moonshine which is Hand Crafted from 100% California Central Valley soft white wheat and bottled at 49.5% abv.

COLORADO

BLACK CANYON DISTILLER
13710 Deere Court, Unit B
Longmont, CO 80504
Tel: (720) 204-1909
Email: fred@blackcanyondistillery.com
www.blackcanyondistillery.com

This family run distillery produces Black Canyon Whiskey which is a sour mash corn whiskey. They also produce Black Canyon Rita which is a pre-made cocktail blend of their whiskey with lime juice, orange juice, mint and cilantro.

BOATHOUSE DISTILLERY
6573 Ridge Rd.
Salida, CO 81201
Email: jmallett123@yahoo.com

They are expecting to complete construction and begin distilling by the Fall of 2012. They will be producing whiskeys made from barley, wheat and rye which will be aged in 5, 15, 30 and 53 gallon barrels from anywhere from 6 months to two years.

BRECKENRIDGE DISTILLERY
1925 Airport Rd.
Breckenridge, CO 80424
Tel: (970) 439-5120
Email: bryantnolt@hotmail.com
www.breckenridgedistillery.com

They produce Breckenridge Bourbon with a mash bill of 56% Yellow Corn, 38% Green Rye, 6% unmalted barley, aged between two and three years in new American white oak barrels. They *also produce a Single Malt Whiskey, and a Spiced Whiskey.*

COLORADO GOLD DISTILLERY
P.O. Box 728
1290 South Grand Mesa Dr.
Cedaredge, CO 81413
Tel: (970) 856-2600
Email: Coop1@kaycee.net
www.coloradogolddistillery.com
Founded in 2007 Colorado Gold produces Colorado Gold Straight Bourbon Whiskey and Colorado's Own Corn Whiskey along with a few other spirits.

DANCING PINES DISTILLERY
1527 Taurus Court #110
Loveland, CO 80537
Tel: (970) 635-3426
Email: info@dpdistillery.com
www.dancingpinesdistillery.com
Among a wide variety of spirits they produce a Bourbon Whiskey made from corn, rye and malted barley. It is twice distilled and aged less than four years in new American white oak casks.

DEERHAMMER DISTILLING COMPANY
Box 1126
321 East Main St.
Buena Vista, CO 81211
Tel: (719) 395-9464
Email: info@deerhammer.com
www.deerhammer.com
This new family owned distillery in the Arkansas River Valley produces Whitewater Whiskey, and just began an annual, limited release of Down Time Single Malt Whiskey.

DISTILLERY 291
1647 S. Tejon St.
Colorado Springs, CO 80919
Tel: (212) 217-9125
Email: info@distillery291.com
www.291coloradowhiskey.com
They produce three whiskeys and are working on a fourth. 291 Colorado Rye Whiskey White Dog has a grain bill of 61% malted rye, 39% corn and briefly placed in a charred American oak barrel before bottling. 291 Colorado Whiskey has the same grain bill as the Rye Whisky but is aged in 5 and 10 gallon barrels for between 6 and 12 months. 291 Fresh Colorado Whiskey has a grain bill of 80% corn and 20% rye and bottled without aging. They are currently working on 291 American Whiskey which will have the same grain bill as the Fresh Colorado Whiskey but aged for 6 months in a 53 gallon charred American oak barrel.

DOWNSLOPE DISTILLING
6770 South Dawson Cir., Ste. 400
Centennial, CO 80112
Tel: (303) 693-4300
Email: spirits@downslopedistilling.com
www.downslopedistilling.com
They produce a variety of spirits including Double Diamond Whiskey which is an Irish style whiskey, made from malted barley and rye, aged in very small toasted oak casks. They are also working on a single malt that will be slightly peaty and aged like the Double Diamond Whiskey.

IRON HORSE DISTILLING
111 Mapel Lane
Durango, CO 81301
Tel: (970) 382-1301
Email: neil@ironhorsedistilling.com
www.ironhorsedistilling.com
This new distillery will be attempting to produce a unique Colorado style whiskey, but they have not said what that means exactly.

JF STROTHMAN DISTILLERY INC
2862 North Ave.
Grand Junction, CO 81501
Tel: (970) 214-2010
Email: wendel@jfstrothmandistillery.com
www.jfstrothmandistillery.com
This Colorado distillery relies heavily on Colorado Olathe Sweet Corn for its Vodka, Bourbon, Corn Whiskey, Moonshine and White Lightning. Their Single Malt Whiskey is made from 2 row and 6 row malted barley.

LEOPOLD BROS.
4950 Nome St., Unit E
Denver, CO 80239
Tel: (303) 307-1515
Email: distiller@leopoldbros.com
www.leopoldbros.com
Leopold Bros. whiskey products include: American Small Batch Whiskey, made from a sour mash of corn and rye, then pot distilled and barreled at 98 proof; New York Apple Whiskey combines their whiskey with fresh juice from apples grown in New York State and then ages this mixture in ex-Bourbon barrels. Leopold Brothers repeats this process for their Rocky Mountain Blackberry, Rocky Mountain Peach and Georgia Peach whiskies.

45th Parallel Spirits | Wisconsin

45TH PARALLEL SPIRITS While whiskey production began in 2009, much of it went to contracts. They are close to releasing some of the whiskey that they produced for themselves, including a bourbon in August 2012, a rye whiskey in the fall of 2012 and a wheat whiskey in the winter. Each will be a straight whiskey, aged between 2 and 3 years in 53 gallon oak casks. Some of the whiskey will continue to age for a few more years for a 4 year release. All their corn, rye and wheat is sourced from a local farm and the spent grain is used as cattle feed.[page 121]

MYSTIC MOUNTAIN DISTILLERY
11505 Valley Rd.
Larkspur, CO 80118
Tel: (303) 633-9375
Email: mysticmt@hotmail.com
www.mysticmtnspirits.com

Besides vodka and gin this distillery also produces two types of whiskey: Rocky Mountain Moonshine Sippin' Hooch is distilled three times, proofed down, charcoal filtered and bottled at 80 and 100 proof; Aces High Bourbon Whiskey is distilled five times, proofed down, charcoal filtered, aged in oak barrels and bottled at 80 proof.

PEACH ST. DISTILLERS
144 S. Kluge Ave., Bldg. #2
Box 87
Palisade, CO 81526
Tel: (970) 464 1128
dave@skabrewing.com
www.peachSt.distillers.com

Along with other products they produce Peach St. Distillers' Colorado Straight Bourbon Whiskey, which is aged for 2 years and bottled at 46% abv. They claim that their whiskey is Colorado's first legal bourbon made in the state.

STRANAHAN'S COLORADO WHISKEY
2405 Blake St.
Denver, CO 80205
Tel: (303) 296 7440
Email: info@stranahans.com
www.stranahans.com

Stranahan's Distillery makes Stranahan's Colorado Whiskey which is made from 100% local malted barley and aged in charred new American oak barrels between two and five years before bottling. They also produce their limited edition Snowflake Series which are finished in a variety of different used wine and liquor barrels.

TRAIL TOWN DISTILLERY
240 Palomino Trail Unit A
Ridgway, CO 81432
Tel: (970) 626-3060
Email: still@trailtownstill.com
www.trailtownstill.com

They produce Coyote Whiskey which is made from 100% local corn. They distill the corn mash to 160 proof then age it with local toasted oak for a few days and bottle it at 45% abv.

VILLAGE DISTILLERY
412 Violet St.
Golden, CO 80401
Tel: (303) 993-7174
Email: s.gould@gouldglobal.com
www.village-distillery.com

Besides a Gin and Absinth they are also currently working on a Whiskey.

CONNECTICUT

ELM CITY DISTILLERY
45 R Ozick Dr. Unit 7
Durham, Ct 06512
Tel: (203) 285-8830
Email: Built into their website
www.elmcitydistillery.com

While they currently offer a vodka they are planning on releasing Nine Square Rye which will be an unaged rye whiskey.

ONYX SPIRITS COMPANY
640 Hilliard St., Suite 3104
Manchester, CT 06042
Tel: (860) 550-1939
Email: contact@onyxspirits.com
www.onyxspirits.com

Touted as the first legal moonshine in New England, Onyx Moonshine, made from corn, malted barley and other grains, was selected as the official spirit in the 2012 GRAMMY Awards. Onyx Spirits was recognized as New England's Best Micro-Distillery after being open only seven months.

DELAWARE

LEGACY DISTILLING
Smyrna, DE 19977
Email: mike@legacydistilling.com

While still in the early start-up phase, Legacy Distilling plans to make at least three types of whiskey. Initially they plan to produce a Bourbon with high rye content, aged in smaller barrels that allow for faster maturation while aging larger barrels between two and twelve years. They want to produce a rye whiskey and corn whiskey aged similarly to the bourbon. They also want to experiment with whiskies made from other grains.

Blue Ridge Distilling | North Carolina

BLUE RIDGE DISTILLING Founded in 2011, production of a single malt whisky began June 2012. [page 105]

FLORIDA

FLAGLER SPIRITS
23 Hargrove Grade, Suite B
Palm Coast, FL 32137
Tel: (386) 986-0641
Email: flaglerspirits@gmail.com
www.flaglerspirits.com
They plan to produce Lightning Corn Whiskey and Spirit Whiskey at 80 and 125 proof.

FLORIDA FARM DISTILLERS
Box 1070
Umatilla, FL 32784
Tel: (352) 455-7232
Email: whiskey@palmridgereserve.com
www.palmridgereserve.com
The make Palm Ridge Reserve Handmade Micro Batch Florida Whiskey which is a bourbon style whisky matured in small charred oak barrels. Currently they only produce 500 bottles of their whiskey per year.

SAINT AUGUSTINE DISTILLING COMPANY
51 Water St.
St. Augustine, FL 32084
Tel: (904) 806-1440
Email: philipalthermcdaniel@gmail.com
They are currently in the advanced planning stages and working on their permitting. Once they are up in running they are looking to make a bourbon with Florida grown corn and soft red winter wheat. They would like to age their spirits in 10 to 30 gallon barrels between 18 months and 3 years depending on how it develops.

GEORGIA

AMERICAN SPIRIT WHISKEY
2633 Birchwood Dr.
Atlanta, GA 30305
Tel: (404) 590-2279
Email: jim@americanspiritwhiskey.com
www.americanspiritwhiskey.com
They produce American Spirit Whiskey which is a blend of new make bourbon and neutral grain spirits, briefly stored in oak and then "ultra-filtered."

GEORGIA DISTILLING COMPANY
121 Blandy Way
Milledgeville, GA 31061
Tel: (404) 281-5484
Email: shawn.hall@georgiadistilling.com
www.georgiadistilling.com
This fairly new distillery makes a vodka and Goodtime Moonshine.

THIRTEENTH COLONY DISTILLERY
305 North. Dudley St.
Americus, GA 31709
Tel: (229) 924-3310
gklemann@13colony.net
www.13colony.net
Georgia's first legal distillery released 13th Colony Southern Corn Whiskey in the fall of 2010 and won a 2011 Gold Medal at the San Francisco World Spirits Competition.

ILLINOIS

FEW SPIRITS
918 Chicago Ave
Evanston, IL 60202
Tel: (847) 920-8628
Email: info@fewspirits.com
fewspirits.com
They currently produce three whiskeys: Few White Whiskey, made from corn and wheat; Few Rye Whiskey, made from rye and corn; Few Bourbon Whiskey, made from corn, rye and malted barley all of which are aged in new charred American oak barrels.

QUINCY STREET DISTILLERY
39 East Quincy St.
Riverside, IL 60546
Tel: (708) 870-5987
Email: manager@quincystreetdistillery.com
www.quincystreetdistillery.com
They are working on producing Water Tower White Lightning, which will be an unaged Illinois corn whiskey. They are owned and operated by Blue Star Potables.

SOUTHERN SISTERS SPIRITS
428 Wood Rd.
Carbondale, IL 62901
Tel: (618) 503-9050
Email: southernsistersspirits@frontier.com
They plan to make a few different types of whiskey including a bourbon. They are developing an apple whiskey in homage to all of the local apple orchards, as well as young whiskeys from wheat, millet and rye aged for less than one year in 30-gallon barrels.

INDIANA

HEARTLAND DISTILLERS
(Colglazier & Hobson Distilling Co.)
9402 Uptown Dr., Suite 1000
Indianapolis, IN 46256
Tel: 317-714-4138
Email: stuart@heartlanddistillers.com
www.heartlanddistillers.com
While they currently have a few different bourbons in development their flagship Spring Mill Indiana Straight Bourbon which has been twice barreled in new charred American white oak and bottled at 45% abv.

OLD POGUE DISTILLERY
7600 Old State St.
Evansville, IN 47710
Tel: (812) 857-6041
Email: info@oldpogue.com
www.oldpogue.com
They produce Old Pogue Master's Select Kentucky Straight Bourbon Whiskey.

IOWA

BROADBENT DISTILLERY
6175 50th Ave.
Norwalk, IA 50211
Tel: (515) 981-0011
Email: john@twojaysiowa.com
www.twojaysiowa.com
Self described as the smallest "legal" micro distillery in Iowa they produce a grappa and two whiskey products: Two Jay's Iowa Corn Whisky, made from 100% local corn and twice distilled; Two Jay's Iowa Corn Whisky Country Style, uses the same whiskey base but it has been aged over toasted oak.

CEDER RIDGE VINEYARDS WINERY & DISTILLER
1441 Marak Rd.
Swisher, IA 52338
Tel: (319) 857-4300
Email: info@crwine.com
www.crwine.com
Along with wine and wide variety of spirits they produce Iowa Bourbon Whiskey, made from a mash of corn, barley and rye, distilled, charcoal filtered and aged. They are currently maturing a single malt whiskey that should be ready for release in 2013.

TEMPLETON RYE
206 East 3rd St.
Templeton, IA 51463
Tel: (617) 233 4893
Email: info@templeton.com
www.templetonrye.com
The Templeton Distillery produces Templeton Prohibition Era Recipe Small Batch Rye Whiskey. Their rye whisky consist of over 90% rye and the balance is malted barley. They double distill and age the whiskey for four years in 53-gallon barrels made of new charred Missouri oak.

MISSISSIPPI RIVER DISTILLING COMPANY
303 North Cody Rd.
Le Claire, IA 52753
Tel: (563) 484-4342
Email: info@mrdistilling.com
www.mrdistilling.com
Among other products they produce River Boat Artisan Spirit which is a new make spirit made from corn and wheat. They also make Cody Rd. Bourbon Whiskey which is made from locally grown corn and regionally sourced wheat and barley, then aged in small new charred American oak from Iowa and Illinois, then bottled at 45% abv. Their recent seasonal spirit was Queen Bee Honey Flavored Whiskey which blended local honey with their aged corn whisky.

KANSAS

DARK HORSE DISTILLERY
11740 West 86th Terrace
Lenexa, KS 66214
Tel: (913) 492-3275
Email: info@dhdistillery.com
www.dhdistillery.com
They are currently distilling a new make spirit called Long Shot White Whiskey which they also plan to age into a Bourbon.

HIGH PLAINS INC
1700 Rooks Rd.
Atchison, KS 66002
Tel: (913) 773 5780
Email: Highplains@highplainsinc.com
www.highplainsinc.com
Founded in 2005 this family distillery has released Most Wanted Pioneer Whiskey and Most Wanted Kansas Bourbon Mash Whiskey.

KENTUCKY

ALLTECH'S BREWING & DISTILLING CO.
401 Cross St.
Lexington, KY 40508
Tel: (859) 255-2337
Email: kentuckyale@alltech.com
www.kentuckyale.com
Alltech Brewing & Distilling is currently aging an unreleased single malt whiskey.

BARREL HOUSE DISTILLING CO.
1200 Manchester St., Bldg. 9
Lexington, KY 40504
Tel: (859) 259 0159
Email: barrelhousedistillery@yahoo.com
www.barrelhousedistillery.com
They produce Devil John Moonshine No. 9 which is made from a mash of corn and sugar and bottled at 45% abv.

CORSAIR ARTISAN DISTILLERY
400 East Main St., #100
Bowling Green, KY 42101
Tel: (615) 400-0056
Email: Andrew@corsairartisan.com
www.corsairartisan.com
Corsair Artisan Distillery produces Wry Moon Unaged Rye Whiskey; a Triple Smoked Whiskey, which is malted barley smoked over cherry, peat, and Beachwood; they have also created a variety of interesting experimental whiskeys.

LIMESTONE BRANCH DISTILLERY
1280 Veterans Memorial Hwy.,
Lebanon, KY, 40033
Tel: (270) 699 9004
Email: info@limestonebranch.com
www.limestonebranch.com
They currently produce 375ml bottles of T.J Pottinger Moon*Shine Kentucky Corn Whiskey

MB ROLAND DISTILLERY
137 Barkers Mill Rd.
Pembroke, KY 42266
Tel: (270) 640 7744
Email: info@mbrdistillery.com
www.mbrdistillery.com
They make a number of different whiskey products. Their White and Black Dog whiskies are made from locally grown white corn. The Black Dog, roasts the corn to give it a smoky character. Their True Kentucky Shine is distilled from a mash of corn and sugar, bottled straight or in three other fruit flavors. They also have a bourbon whiskey that is currently aging in oak barrels.

SILVER TRAIL DISTILLERY
136 Palestine Rd.,
Hardin, KY, 42048
Tel: (270) 354-9657
They are currently using an eighty year old family recipe to make 100 proof Corn Whiskey in a rare square pot still with two condensers. They also have plans to make a Pineapple Shine, an Apple Shine and LBLX Bourbon.

LOUISIANA

DONNER-PELTIER DISTILLERS
1635 St. Patrick Hwy.
Thibodaux, LA 70301
Tel: (985) 413-3700
Email: hpeltier@charter.net
www.dp-distillers.com
They are planning to make bourbon with corn, rye, and barley aged in American oak barrels for 3-5 years.

MAINE

NEW ENGLAND DISTILLING
26 Evergreen Dr. Unit B
Portland, ME 04103
Tel: (207) 878-9759
Email: info@newenglanddistilling.com
www.newenglanddistilling.com
Along with their Gin they are currently working on a Rye Whiskey, which has a mash bill that is mostly rye and some barley. Currently the are aging the rye in 10 to 30-gallon barrels. They also have plans to work on a variety of other whiskey styles like bourbon, single malt, as well as whiskeys made from uncommon grains.

SWEETGRASS FARM DISTILLERY
325 Carroll Rd.
Union, ME 04862
Tel: (207) 785-3042
Email: info@sweetgrasswinery.com
www.sweetgrasswinery.com
Operating since 2005, they are in their second year of whiskey production. They are currently making a single malt whiskey from Maine grown barley which will age for about 8 years before it is released.

MARYLAND

BLACKWATER DISTILLING
184 Log Canoe Cir.
Stevensville, MD 21666
Tel: (443) 249-3123
Email: press@sloopbetty.com
www.blackwaterdistilling.com
While this new distillery is currently producing a vodka they have plans to start making whiskey too.

NEW COLUMBIA DISTILLERS
7000 Hillcrest Place
Chevy Chase, MD 20815
Email: cheers@greenhatgin.com
www.greenhatgin.com
www.newcolumbiadistillers.com
While still in the construction phase, their first product is slated to be Green Hat Gin but they also plan to produce a rye whiskey.

MASSACHUSETTS

BERKSHIRE MOUNTAIN DISTILLERS
1640 Home Rd.
Great Barrington, MA 01230
Tel: (413) 429-6280
Email: chris@berkshiremountaindistillers.com
www.berkshiremountaindistillers.com
Established in 2007, they are producing Berkshire Bourbon made from locally sources corn, and New England Corn Whiskey which is made from the same local corn and aged over oak and cherry wood from their farm.

BULLY BOY DISTILLERS
35 Cedric St.
Boston, MA 02119
Tel: (617) 442-6000
Email: info@bullyboydistillers.com
www.bullyboydistillers.com
They produce Bully Boy White Whiskey, and Bully Boy Wheat Whiskey which uses organic red winter wheat as its primary ingredient. Both whiskies are USDA certified organic.

DAMNATION ALLEY DISTILLERY
19 Jones Court, Unit 3
Newton, MA 02458
Tel: (617) 669-6756
Email: info@damnationalleydistillery.com
www.damnationalleydistillery.com
While they are not currently open yet they plan on making a white whiskey.

NASHOBA DISTILLERY
100 Wattaquadoc Hill Rd.
Bolton, MA 01740
Tel: (978) 779-5521
Email: email@nashobawinery.com
www.nashobawinery.com
Established in 2003 as Massachusetts' first farm distillery, they produce Stimulus Single Malt American Whiskey, which is made for 100% malted barley and aged for 5 years in new and used oak barrels.

RYAN & WOOD DISTILLERIES
15 Great Republic Dr. U-2
Gloucester, MA 01930
Tel: (978) 281-2282
Email: info@ryanandwood.com
ryanandwood.com
They produce Ryan & Wood Straight Rye Whiskey, which is made from a mash of rye, wheat and barley, distilled on the grain and aged for at least two years in new charred American White Oak barrels.

TRIPLE EIGHT DISTILLERY
Box 2928
5 Bartlett Farm Rd.
Nantucket, MA 02554
Tel: (508) 325-5929
Email: jay@ciscobrewers.com
www.ciscobrewers.com
Triple Eight produces a Scottish style single malt whiskey known as Notch, so called because it is "not Scotch." Notch is made from a mash of Maris Otter malt, distilled, and aged for 8 years in ex-bourbon barrels and finished in French oak merlot casks from Nantucket Vineyards. They also produce Nor'Easter Bourbon, made primarily from a corn mash, aged in new charred American oak barrels.

MICHIGAN

CIVILIZED SPIRITS
13512 Peninsula Dr.
Traverse City, MI 49686
Tel: (231) 223-4222
Email: info@northernunitedbrewing.com
www.civilizedspirits.com
Among other spirits they produce three versions of their Civilized Whiskey. Their standard whiskey is made from locally grown rye and aged in white oak barrels. Their White Dog Whiskey is made from locally grown rye and wheat and bottled at 40% abv. Their Civilized Single Malt Whiskey is made from peated malted barley that is aged in oak barrels for 3 years in their climate controlled rick house.

GRAND TRAVERSE DISTILLERY
781 Industrial Cir., Suite 5
Traverse City, MI 49686
Tel: (231) 947-8635
Email: info@grandtraversedistillery.com
www.grandtraversedistillery.com
They produce Ole George 100% Straight Rye Whiskey which is aged for at least two years and bottled straight from the barrel at 93 proof.

JOURNEYMAN DISTILLERY
109 Generations Dr.
Three Oaks, MI 49128
Tel: (269) 820-2050
Email: info@journeymandistillery.com
www.journeymandistillery.com
They produce a wide variety of organic whiskies. Their first product came off the still in 2010 and is called Ravenswood Rye Whiskey which is made from Michigan wheat and Minnesota rye and aged in 15-gallon new charred white oak barrels. W.R. Whiskey is a white whiskey made from the same mash bill as the Ravenswood and aged for 24 hours in new white oak. Buggy Whip Wheat Whiskey is made from organic wheat but has no age statement. Featherbone Bourbon Whiskey and Michigan Spirit Whiskey are slated to be released later in 2012, the spirit whiskey is a blend 80% spirit and 20% aged whiskey. Their newest product Three Oaks Single Malt are aging in three different barrels and scheduled to be released in 2013.

NEW HOLLAND BREWING COMPANY
66 East 8th St.
Holland, MI 49423
Tel: (616)355-6422
Email: brett@newhollandbrew.com
www.newhollandbrew.com
They produce six whiskey products: Walleye Rye Whiskey, made from malted rye and 2-row barley; Malthouse Whiskey, made from 2-row, smoked barley and rye; Double Down Barley Whiskey, is made from 100% 2-row malted barley and aged in 5 gallon barrels; Bill's Single Barrel Wheat is a special wheated whiskey aged in 15-gallon barrels for 36 months; Zeppelin Bend Straight Malt Whiskey; Hatter Royale Hopquila is made from 100% barley distilled twice and steeped with Centennial Hops.

MINNESOTA

PANTHER DISTILLERY
300 East Pike St.
Osakis, MN 56360
Tel: (320) 815-0484
Email: pantherdistillery@gmail.com
www.pantherdistillery.com
Currently they produce White Water Whiskey which is made from a bourbon whisky mash of locally gown corn and red wheat. They also have three whiskeys maturing with a planed release in 2014. Their Ironwood Whiskey is made from Minnesota red wheat and yellow corn. Their Red Rye Whiskey is made from 100% locally gown rye and aged in charred oak barrels. Their Blue Earth Bourbon is made from the same grain bill as their White Water Whiskey.

MISSOURI

COPPER RUN DISTILLERY
1901 Day Rd.
Walnut Shade, MO 65771
Tel: (417) 294-0375
jimdblansit@aol.com
www.copperrundistillery.com
Touted as the first legal distillery in Missouri, they produce Copper Run Moonshine and Copper Run Spirit Whiskey.

CROWN VALLEY BREWING & DISTILLING
13326 State Route F
Ste. Genevieve, MO 63670
Tel: (573) 756-9700
Email: info@crownvalleybrewery.com
www.crowncountry.com
Their Missouri Moonshine is made from a mash of rye and barley.

MAD BUFFALO DISTILLING
Shawnee Bend Farms
7616 Shawneetown Spur
Union, MO 63084
Tel: (423) 457-9809
Email: info@madbuffalodistillery.com
www.madbuffalodistillery.com
This farm distillery is beginning its whiskey production with Thunder Beast 100% Corn Whiskey, which will be aged between six to eight months in 15-gallon white Missouri oak barrels. They also plan to make a bourbon that will be aged for about a year in similar barrels with a medium char. They will also produce Moonshine, which will be an unaged version of their 100% corn whiskey.

Death's Door Spirits | Wisconsin

Death's Door Spirits Along with vodka and gin they produce Death's Door White Whisky, which they make from 80% organic Washington Island Wheat and 20% organic malted barley from Chilton, Wisconsin. [page 121]

They plan to grow and malt all of the corn that goes into their whiskeys.

PINCKNEY BEND DISTILLERY
1101B Miller St. Box 15
New Haven, MO 63068
Tel: (573) 237-5559
Email: Built into their website
www.pinckneybend.com
They are currently aging Pinckney Bend Whiskey.

SPIRITS OF ST. LOUIS
1727 Park Ave
St. Louis, MO 63104
Tel: (314) 231-2537
Email: info@squareonebrewery.com
www.squareonebrewery.com
They produce J.J. Neukomm Whiskey which is made with cherry wood smoked malt and aged in Midwest made oak barrels. They also produce Vermont Night which is an oak aged Whiskey liqueur, sweetened with Vermont maple syrup.

MONTANA

GLACIER DISTILLING COMPANY
Box 593
West Glacier, MT 59936
Tel: (406) 387-9887
Email: info@glacierdistilling.com
www.glacierdistilling.com
They are producing five whisky products: Wheatfish Whiskey, made from a mash bill of Montana grown wheat and barley and briefly aged in oak; Bad Rock Rye Whiskey is a rye based whiskey that is bottled one barrel at a time; North Fork Flood State Whiskey has a mash bill of rye, barley and corn which is aged in charred American oak; North Fork On The Fly takes their aged North Fork whiskey and infuses it with fresh cut peaches.

HEADFRAME SPIRITS
21 South Montana St.
Butte, MT 59701
Tel: (406) 299-2886
Email: cheers@headframespirits.com
www.headframespirits.com
They produce two whiskeys: Neversweat Bourbon Whiskey and Destroying Angel Whiskey which are both named after mining sites in Butte.

ROUGHSTOCK DISTILLERY
705 Osterman Dr., Suite C
Bozeman, MT 59715
Tel: (406) 579-3986
Email: bryan@montanawhiskey.com
www.montanawhiskey.com
They produce five whiskeys: Rough Stock Montana Whiskey is made from 100% locally grown barley and aged in lightly charred new American oak barrels; Black Label Montana Whiskey is the limited edition single barrel, cask strength version of their standard whiskey; Spring Wheat Whiskey is made from 100% locally grown hard white spring wheat and aged in their ex-malt barrels; Sweet Corn Whiskey is made from 100% locally grown sweet yellow corn and bottled with out aging at 50% abv; Straight Rye Whiskey is made from 100% rye and aged for at least two years in charred new American oak barrels.

WHISTLING ANDY
8541 Hwy. 35
Bigfork, MT 5991
Tel: (406) 551-6409
Email: andy@whistlingandy.com
www.whistlingandy.com
Among other products they are producing Whistling Andy Moonshine, which is made from Montana barley, winter wheat, rye and corn.

NEBRASKA

COOPER'S CHASE DISTILLERY
584 18th Rd.
West Point, NE 68788
Tel: (402) 380-0233
Email: Built into their website
www.cooperschase.com
While their only available product at present is their Chase Vodka they have plans to produce a bourbon and a corn whiskey.

SÒLAS DISTILLERY
11941 Centennial Rd. Ste. 1
La Vista, NE 68128
Tel: (402) 763-8868
Email: info@solasdistillery.com
www.jossvodka.com
Founded in 2005, they are currently working on barrel aged Scottish style single malt whiskey.

Kings County Distillery | New York

Kings County Distillery Founded in 2010 they produce both moonshine and a bourbon whiskey. [page 104]

NEVADA

CHURCHILL VINEYARDS & DISTILLERY
1045 Dodge Lane
Fallon, NV 89406
Tel: (775) 423-4000
Email: info@churchillvineyards.com
www.churchillvineyards.com
Their Nevada Single Malt Whiskey is distilled from malted barley grown on the historic Frey Ranch in Fallon, Nevada.

LAS VEGAS DISTILLERY
7330 Eastgate Rd. #100
Henderson, NV 89011
Tel: (702) 629-7534
Email: info@lasvegasdistillery.com
www.lasvegasdistillery.com
Their Whiskey Smith series includes 14 different expressions of whiskey! They also produce something they call Rumskey which is distilled from a mash of 50% fermented molasses and 50% fermented whiskey grains.

TAHOE BLÜ DISTILLERY
Box 10796
Reno, NV 89510
Tel: (775) 315-1787
Email: info@tahoebludistillery.com
www.tahoebludistillery.com
They make Tahoe Blu Single Malt Whiskey which is made from 100% malted barley.

NEW JERSEY

COOPER RIVER DISTILLERS
38 North 4th St.
Camden, NJ 08102
Tel: (267) 469-7739
Email: james@cooperriverdistillers.com
www.cooperriverdistillers.com
They planned to begin production in Fall 2012 and to begin selling their whiskeys in 2013. They plan to produce four whiskeys: Silver Fox White Rye Whiskey, an unaged rye whiskey made from about 10% malted barley, 10% malted rye with the rest unmalted rye and sourced from local South Jersey farms; A naked bourbon, which will be an unaged whiskey based on a bourbon mash, and as yet unnamed; Aged bourbon & rye whiskeys which will mature using a mix of small (10-15 gallon) and larger barrels (30-60 gallons).

NEW MEXICO

DON QUIXOTE DISTILLERY
236 Rio Bravo
Los Alamos, NM 87544
Tel: (505) 695-0817
Email: Built into their website
www.dqdistillery.com
They make Don Quixote Blue Corn Bourbon, which is made from 75% New Mexico organic blue corn, 23% wheat and 2% barley, and aged in new charred American oak barrels for 4 years.

SANTA FE SPIRITS
7505 Mallard Way, Unit 1
Santa Fe, NM 87507
Tel: (505) 467-8892
Email: info@santafespirits.com
www.santafespirits.com
They produce two whiskeys: Silver Coyote Pure Malt Whiskey is a combination of Scottish yeast, European and American malts; Their Santa Fe Spirits' Single Malt Whiskey is made entirely from malted barley, and aged in various oak casks to enhance its flavor profile.

NEW YORK

BREUCKELEN DISTILLING COMPANY
77 19th St.
Brooklyn, NY 11232
Tel: (347) 725-4985
Email: info@brkdistilling.com
www.brkdistilling.com
They produce, 77 Whiskey which is distilled from 100% New York wheat, and aged a minimum of 4 months in new American Oak; Their 77 Whiskey (rye) is distilled from 90% Rye and 10% Corn, both locally sourced and aged a minimum of 7 months in new American Oak.

CATSKILL DISTILLING COMPANY
2037 Route 17B
Bethel, NY 12720
Tel: (845) 583-8569
Email: Info@CatskillDistilling.com
www.catskilldistilling.com
They produce a wide variety of whiskey products including White Whiskey, Corn Whiskey, Wheat Whiskey, Rye Whiskey, Buckwheat Whiskey, Bourbon, with rye, and Bourbon with wheat, aged in new heavy charred American oak.

COPPERSEA DISTILLERY
P.O. Box 204
West Park, NY 12493
Tel: (845) 444-1044
Email: michael@coppersea.com
www.coppersea.com
While they are currently finalizing their licensing, they do plan to produce a bourbon, a rye whiskey, and a Scottish style malt whiskey. They plan to age their whiskies in a combination of new oak and used wine barrels.

DELAWARE PHOENIX DISTILLERY
Box 245
144 Delaware St.
Walton, NY 13856
Tel: (607) 865-5056
Email: cheryllins@frontiernet.net
www.delawarephoenix.com
They are currently producing three types of whiskey. Their bourbon, corn and rye whiskeys were released around Thanksgiving 2011.

FINGER LAKES DISTILLING
4676 NYS Route 414
Burdett, NY 14818
Tel: (607) 546-5510
Email: brian@fingerlakesdistilling.com
www.fingerlakesdistilling.com
They produce five types of whiskey. McKenzie Bourbon Whiskey is a double-pot distilled bourbon made from a local, heirloom variety of corn that makes up 70% of the mash bill and is aged in 10-gallon, new charred barrels and finish in local Chardonnay casks; McKenzie Rye Whiskey is made from NYS grain, aged in new charred quarter casks and finished in sherry barrels from local wineries; McKenzie Pure Pot Still Whiskey is their take on an Irish-style whiskey that uses a combination of locally-grown unmalted and malted barley. The whiskey is aged in their used bourbon and rye barrels and bottled at 80 proof; Glen Thunder is an American corn whiskey, made to honor the Watkins Glen International Raceway; White Pike Whiskey is a young whiskey made from a mash of locally grown corn, spelt and malted wheat then aged in oak for 18 minutes before bottling.

HIDDEN MARSH DISTILLERY
2981 Auburn Rd.
Seneca Falls, NY 13148
Tel: (315) 568-8190
Email: info@beevodka.com
www.beevodka.com
Along with their honey vodka they make Judd's Wreckin' Ball Corn Whiskey.

HILLROCK ESTATE DISTILLERY
408 Pooles Hill Road
Ancram, NY 12502
Tel: (518) 329-1023
Email: info@hillrockdistillery.com
http://hillrockdistillery.com
Distillation at the estate commenced in October 2011 and they have released the Hillrock Solera Aged Bourbon Whiskey. Besides corn the mash bill is about 37% rye, and the bourbon has an average age of 6 years before being bottled at 46.3% abv. They are in the process of ageing the soon to be released Estate Single Malt and Estate Rye whiskeys which will be made from organic barley and rye grown and malted at the Hillrock Estate.

KINGS COUNTY DISTILLERY
Brooklyn Navy Yard, Bldg. 121
63 Flushing Ave., Box 379
Brooklyn, NY 11205
Email: info@kingscountydistillery.com
www.kingscountydistillery.com
Founded in 2010 they produce both moonshine and a bourbon whiskey.

NAHMIAS ET FILS
201 Saw Mill River Rd. Bldg. C
Yonkers, NY 10701
Tel: (646) 644-4256
Email: info@nahmiasetfils.com
www.nahmiasetfils.com
They produce Legs Diamond Rye Whiskey, which is made with rye grown on locally sustainable farms. The whiskey is named after Legs Diamond, a famous bootlegger during prohibition who operated in and around New York City.

NEW YORK DISTILLING COMPANY
79 Richardson St.
Brooklyn, NY 11211
Tel: (718) 965-0022
Email: info@nydistilling.com
www.nydistilling.com
While they currently produce two styles of gin they have plans to make American Rye Whiskey.

SARATOGA DISTILLERIES
2474 Old Mill Rd.
Galway, NY 12074
Tel: (518) 584-8521
Email: corporate@saratogadistilleries.com
www.saratogadistilleries.com
They currently are the only distillers working in Saratoga and they produce both corn and rye Whiskeys.

THE NOBLE EXPERIMENT NYC
23 Meadow St.
Brooklyn, NY 11206
Tel: 917 705-6755
Email: info@tnenyc.com
www.tnenyc.com
Along with rum they are producing bourbon and rye whiskeys distilled from 100% New York grown grains.

TIRADO DISTILLERY
888 East 163 St.
Bronx, NY 10459
Tel: (917) 974-0380
Email: madhern@yahoo.com
www.tiradorum.com
Touted as the first distillery to operate legally in the Bronx since Prohibition, they produce Tirado Gold Corn Whiskey and an unaged corn whiskey.

TUTHILLTOWN SPIRITS DISTILLERY
14 Gristmill Lane
Gardiner, NY 12525
Tel: (845) 633-8734
Email: Ralph@tuthilltown.com
www.tuthilltown.com
Founded in 2005, Tuthilltown Spirits expressions include Hudson Baby Bourbon, an unaged Hudson New York Corn Whiskey, Tuthilltown Government Warning Rye, and Tuthilltown Single Malt Whiskey. They are currently owned by William Grant & Sons.

NORTH CAROLINA

ASHEVILLE DISTILLING COMPANY
12 Old Charlotte Hwy. Suite T
Asheville NC 28803
Tel: (828) 575-2000
Email: troy@troyandsons.com
www.troyandsons.com
Founded in 2010, they produce Troy & Sons Moonshine, which is made from Crooked Creek Corn which is an heirloom variety grown locally.

BLUE RIDGE DISTILLING
228 Redbud Lane
Bostic, NC 28018
Tel: (828) 245-2041
Email: info@blueridgedistilling.com
www.blueridgedistilling.com
Founded in 2011, production of a single malt whisky began June 2012.

HOWLING MOON DISTILLERY
42 Old Elk Mountain Rd.
Asheville NC 28804
Tel: (828) 208-1469
Email: info@howlingmoonshine.com
www.howlingmoonshine.com
They make Raymond Fairchild Mountain Moonshine which is made from stone ground local corn.

PIEDMONT DISTILLERS
203 East Murphy St.
Madison, NC 27025
Tel: (336) 445-0055
Email: info@piedmontdistillers.com
www.piedmontdistillers.com
Piedmont distillers produce a variety of moonshine products: Catdaddy Spiced Moonshine which is made from corn and triple distilled; Junior Johnson's Midnight Moon, and a series of Midnight Moon infused with fruit.

TOP OF THE HILL DISTILLERY
505-C West Franklin St.
Chapel Hill, NC 27516
Tel: (919) 929-8676
Email: Built into their website
www.topodistillery.com
Along with vodka and gin they produce TOPO Carolina Whiskey, which is made from organic wheat grown in the Carolinas. They also produce an Age-Your-Own Whiskey Kit which includes two bottles of their whiskey and a small oak barrel. All of their products are certified USDA Organic.

OHIO

MARKET GARDEN BREWERY & DISTILLERY
1947 West 25th St.
Cleveland, OH 44113
Tel: (216) 621-4000
Email: sam.mcnulty@gmail.com
www.marketgardenbrewery.com
While currently waiting for their federal license they do plan on making whiskey. Their whiskey will be made primarily from all malted grain formulas and aged in new barrels. However, some of the whiskey will be aged in used bourbon barrels or used wine barrels for a total of 2 to 4 years. They are also thinking of producing some white whiskey.

Copper Fox | Virginia

Copper Fox Founded in 2000 they produce Wasmund's Single Malt Whiskey, Copper Fox Rye Whiskey, as well as the un-aged Wasmund's Single Malt Spirit and Wasmund's Rye Spirit. They are also working on a Bourbon that is not ready to be bottled. [page 116]

DANCING TREE DISTILLERY
41625 Bearwallow Ridge
Shade, OH 45776
Email: kelly@dancingtreedistillery.com
www.dancingtreedistillery.com
Founded in 2011, they are producing an aged Corn Whiskey that is made from 81% locally sourced organic, non-gmo corn and 19% Briess organic 2-row barley, aged in ex-bourbon barrels for about 24 months.

ERNEST SCARANO DISTILLERY
1989 County Rd. 62
Gibsonburg, OH 43431
Tel: (419) 205-8734
Email: ernie@esdistillery.com
www.esdistillery.com
They are producing Old Homicide Whiskey.

FLAT ROCK SPIRITS
5380 Intrastate Dr.
Fairborn, OH 45324
Tel: (937) 879-4447
Email: james@flatrockspirits.com
www.flatrockspirits.com
They produce small batch bourbon that is currently aging before its release.

INDIAN CREEK DISTILLERY
7095 Staley Rd.
New Carlisle, OH 45344
Tel: (937) 845-1142
Email: Jmduer76@gmail.com
They are producing two rye whiskeys: Staley Rye Whiskey, which is aged in small oak barrels and Revolution Rye Whiskey which is an un-aged expression of their rye. Each style is bottled uncut and they are looking to grow rye on their own farm for the whiskey.

JOHN MCCULLOCH DISTILLERY
P.O. Box 112
Martinsville, Ohio 45146
Tel: (937) 725-5588
Email spirits@greenriverwhiskey.com
www.greenriverwhiskey.com
They produce two whiskey products: Mountain Dew Grain Spirits, which is a pre-prohibition style spirit, and Green River Whiskey.

MIDDLE WEST SPIRITS
1230 Courtland Ave.
Columbus, OH 43201
Tel: (614) 299-2460
Email: info@middlewestspirits.com
www.middlewestspirits.com
Among other spirits they produce OYO Whiskey, which is made from 100% Ohio grown soft red winter wheat and aged in oak.

TOM'S FOOLERY
7150 Country Lane
Chagrin Falls, OH 44023
Tel: (216) 570-5776
Email: tom@tomsfoolery.com
www.applejackohio.com
At the end of 2011 they had installed two historic pot stills and began production of a traditional Sour Mash Bourbon Whiskey that will be aged in new charred American Oak.

WOODSTONE CREEK
3641 Newton Ave.
Cincinnati, OH 45207
Tel: (513) 474-3521
Email: woodstonecreek@yahoo.com
www.woodstonecreek.com
They make a variety whiskies including: Single Barrel Bourbon Whiskey, made from 51% white and yellow corn, with the remainder malted rye, barley and white wheat; a 10-year old Single Peated Malt Whiskey, a Spirit Whiskey, which is a blend of three 8-year old malts and a 3-year old wheat whiskey; Ridge Runner Five Grain Moonshine; Ridge Runner Peat Reek; Single Peated Malt White Dog whiskey among others.

OREGON

BULL RUN DISTILLING
2259 MW Quimby St.
Portland, OR 97210
Tel: (503) 224-3483
Email: Built into their website
www.bullrundistillery.com
Founded in the Spring of 2010, they are currently maturing a Straight Oregon Whiskey that is scheduled for release some time in 2015.

CANNON BEACH DISTILLERY
255 N. Hemlock, Box 264
Cannon Beach, OR 97110
Tel: (503) 440-5462
Email: cannonbeachdistillery@gmail.com
Newly opened in July 2012, they are planning on producing a couple of limited release whiskeys that will be aged in Black Swan, 10-gallon, honeycomb

Dark Corner Distillery | South Carolina

Dark Corner Distillery They produce Dark Corner Distillery Moonshine Corn Whiskey. They also produce three flavored whiskies with their moonshine as the base. [page 111]

barrels for about two years before bottling. Their first product is likely to be bourbon that emphasizes rye and smoked malts

CASCADE PEAK SPIRITS
Box 1198
Ashland, OR 97520
Tel: (541) 482-8077
Email: diane@organicnationspirits.com
www.organicnationspirits.com

They produce OldField Rye Whiskey, which is made from a mash of local organic rye, and organic malt. It is aged in 10-gallon new oak barrels for about 20 months before bottling.

CLEAR CREEK DISTILLERY
2389 NW Wilson
Portland, OR 97210
Tel: (503) 248 9470
Email: steve@clearcreekdistillery.com
www.clearcreekdistillery.com

Clear Creek Distillery produces McCarthy's Oregon Single Malt Whiskey. They use heavy peat malted barley from Scotland that is fermented by the Widmer Brothers Brewery, distilled in one pass and barrel aged in ex-sherry casks and finished in barrels made from air dried Oregon Oak. Their current edition is about 3 years old.

EASTSIDE DISTILLING
1512 SE 7th Ave.
Portland, Oregon 97214
Tel: (503) 926-7060
Email: info@eastsidedistilling.com
www.eastsidedistilling.com

Along with three rums they produce Burnside Bourbon which is a 4-year old Straight Bourbon Whiskey.

HARD TIMES DISTILLERY
175 South 5th St.
Monroe, OR 97448
Tel: (541) 357-8808
Email: Info@hardtimesdistillery.com
www.hardtimesdistillery.com

Founded in late 2009, they produce Sweet Baby Moonshine, which is an unaged sour mash whiskey made from 50% oats, 45% barley and 5% cane sugar, and bottled at 95 proof.

HOUSE SPIRITS DISTILLERY
2025 SE 7th Ave.
Portland, OR 97214
Tel: (503) 235 3174
Email: info@housespirits.com
www.housespirits.com

Founded in 2004, they are producing Westward Small Batch Oregon Straight Malt Whiskey, as well as House Spirits Whiskey, which was released in limited quantity as part of their Stillroom Series.

IMMORTAL SPIRITS & DISTILLING COMPANY
3582 S. Pacific Hwy. #D
Medford, OR 97504
Tel: (541) 646-8144
Email: info@immortalspirits.com
www.immortalspirits.com

They produce a variety of whiskeys including: Early, which is a white whisky form of their bourbon mash; Single Malt Whiskey, which is made with in-house smoked malts from local woods and was slated to be released in December 2012. They are also working on a Black Whiskey, which takes their smoked malt whiskey and mixes it with a proprietary blend of natural ingredients that produce a dark black liquor.

MCMENAMINS CORNELIUS PASS ROADHOUSE DISTILLERY
4045 N.W. Cornelius Pass Rd.
Hillsboro, OR 97124
Tel: (503) 640-6174
Email: distillery@mcmenamins.com
www.mcmenamins.com

This location operates a 100+-year old 160-gallon Alambic Charentais pot still and currently produces White Owl Whiskey, which is a wheat based whiskey bottled straight from the still at 49.3% abv.

MCMENAMINS EDGEFIELD DISTILLERY
2126 SW Halsey St.
Troutdale, OR 97060
Tel: (503) 669-8610
Email: distillery@mcmenamins.com
www.mcmenamins.com

This distillery which opened in 1998 uses a hybrid Holstein still and produces three whiskey products: Monkey Puzzle, which is a dry-hopped version of their malt whiskey sweetened with Edgefield estate blackberry honey; Hogshead Whiskey is made from a mash of four different malted barley grains including chocolate malt and roasted malt; White Dog Whiskey, which is an unaged version of their Hogshead whiskey.

OREGON SPIRIT DISTILLERS
490 Butler Market Rd. Ste. 110
Bend, OR 97701
Tel: (541) 382-0002
Email: info@oregonspiritdistillers.com
www.oregonspiritdistillers.com

This family operated distillery produces C.W. Irwin Straight Bourbon and they are currently working on a rye whiskey.

RANSOM SPIRITS
23101 Houser Rd.
Sheridan, Oregon 97378
Tel: (503) 876-5022
Email: tad@ransomspirits.com
www.ransomspirits.com

Founded in 1997, they produce WhipperSnapper Oregon Spirit Whisky, a blend of unaged Kentucky corn whiskey, which they re-distill and add to their in house barley spirit. This blend is then aged in used French pinot noir barrels, ex-American whiskey casks and new American oak barrels, between six months and two years. Each bottling combines eight barrels for the target profile.

ROGUE DISTILLERIES
Rogue House of Spirits
2122 Marine Science Dr.
Newport, OR
Tel: (541) 867-3670
Rogue Distillery & Public House
1339 NW Flanders
Portland, OR 97209
Tel: (503) 222-5910
Email: brett@rogue.com
www.rogue.com

Their first distillery opened in 2003 and the second in 2006. They produce Dead Guy Whiskey, which is made from the same four malts used in their Dead Guy Ale: Northwest Harrington, Maier Munich, Klages, and Carastan malts. They also produce Chatoe Rogue Oregon Single Malt Whiskey, which is made from Risk™ malt grown on Rogue's Micro Barley Farm in the Tygh Valley.

STEIN DISTILLERY
604 North Main St., Box 200
Joseph, OR 97846
Tel: (503) 642-2659
Email: whiskey@steindistillery.com
www.steindistillery.com

This family owned farm distillery produces a Rye Whiskey from their grain.

STONE BARN BRANDY WORKS
3315 SE 19th Suite B
Portland, OR 97202
Tel: (503) 775-6747
Email: degens@stonebarnbrandyworks.com
www.stonebarnbrandyworks.com

They currently produce three whisky products: Hard Eight Dark Rye Spirits, which is and unaged spirit made from a mash of organic, stone ground dark rye flour, bottled at 40% abv; Hoppin' Eights Whiskey, is a series of single barrel whiskeys made from a variety of grains. They are also working on an un-oaked oat whiskey.

PENNSYLVANIA

MOUNTAIN LAUREL SPIRITS
Building #4
925 Canal St.
Bristol, PA 19007
Tel: (215) 781-8300
Email: info@dadshatrye.com
www.dadshatrye.com

Founded in 2010, they produce Dad's Hat Pennsylvania White Rye and Dad's Hat Pennsylvania Rye Whiskey. Both are made from malted barley and Pennsylvania grown rye, while the whisky is aged in charred American oak quarter casks and stored in a temperature controlled environment.

PHILADELPHIA DISTILLING
12285 McNulty Rd.
Philadelphia, PA 19154
Tel: (215) 671-0346
Email: info@shinewhiskey.com
www.philadelphiadistilling.com

Opened in 2005, they began producing XXX SHINE White (corn) Whiskey in 2011.

PITTSBURGH DISTILLERY
2401 Smallman St.
Pittsburgh, PA 15222
Tel: (412) 224-2827
Email: eric@wiglewhiskey.com
www.wiglewhiskey.com

Opened in 2012, their whiskeys are named after Philip Wiggle who was hung for his participation in the Whiskey Rebellion. They produce two white whiskeys: Wigle Whiskey A Rebellious White Rye, made from local organic rye and malted barley; and Wigle Whiskey A Rebellious White Wheat, made from local organic wheat and malted barley. Both are briefly stored in white oak barrels before bottling so they can be called whiskey. They are also maturing aged versions of their rye and wheat whiskies, using toasted Pennsylvania white oak.

RHODE ISLAND

SONS OF LIBERTY DISTILLERY
1425 Kingstown Rd.
South Kingstown, RI 02879
Tel: (401) 218-9385
Email: info@solspirits.com
www.solspirits.com

Founded in 2010, they produce Uprising American Whiskey which is distilled from a stout beer. They then mature the spirit with oak staves for a little less than one year before bottling to highlight the malt profile of the original beer. Believing that good whiskey come from good beer they are experimenting with a range of seasonal whiskeys based on a variety of seasonal beer styles. Eventually they plan to age their spirits by the ocean in both small and large oak barrels to draw in more local character from the sea air. Finally, they hope to help build and define an American single malt style that can rival Scottish single malts.

SOUTH CAROLINA

DARK CORNER DISTILLERY
241-B North Main St.
Greenville, SC 29601
Tel:(864) 631-1144
Email: joe@darkcornerdistillery.com
www.darkcornerdistillery.com
They produce Dark Corner Distillery Moonshine Corn Whiskey. They also produce three flavored whiskeys with their moonshine as the base.

STRIPED PIG DISTILLERY
2046 S. Smokerise Way
Mt. Pleasant, SC 29466
Tel: (504) 957-2147
Email: todd@stripedpigdistillery.com
www.stripedpigdistillery.com
Founded in 2011, after they finish construction they will begin producing rum and whiskey.

SOUTH DAKOTA

DAKOTA SPIRITS DISTILLERY
3601 Airport Rd.
Pierre, SD 57501
Tel: 605-494-1009
Email: dakotaspiritsdistillery@gmail.com
www.dakotaspirits.com
Touted as South Dakota's first legal distillery, they produce Bickering Brothers Blended Whiskey, which is 50% straight bourbon whiskey and 50% grain spirits. They also make Coyote 100 Light Whiskey, which is briefly aged in American oak to gain some color and flavor.

TENNESSEE

CHATTANOOGA WHISKEY COMPANY
504 East 16th St.
Chattanooga, TN 37408
Tel: (423) 580-5610
Email: Built into their website
www.chattanoogawhiskey.com
They produce 1816 Reserve which is made from a mash bill of 75% corn, 21% rye, and 4% malted barley. The whiskey is aged for three years in charred American white oak barrels and bottled at 45% abv. They also produce a cask strength version called 1816 Cask which is bottled at 56.8% abv.

CORSAIR ARTISAN DISTILLERY
1200 Clinton St. #110
Nashville, TN 37203
Tel: (615) 200-0320
Email: darek@corsairartisan.com
www.corsairartisan.com
Corsair Artisan Distillery produces Wry Moon Unaged Rye Whiskey; a Triple Smoked Whiskey, which is malted barley smoked over cherry, peat, and Beachwood; they have also created a variety of interesting experimental whiskeys.

FUGITIVE SPIRITS
2710 Belmont Blvd.
Nashville, TN 37212
Tel: (615) 830-0043
Email: info@fugitivespirits.com
www.fugitivespirits.com
This new distillery plans to produce a White Dog Whiskey, a regular Whiskey, a Bourbon and a Tennessee Whiskey.

NELSON'S GREEN BRIER DISTILLERY
Nashville, TN
Email: andy@greenbrierdistillery.com
www.greenbrierdistillery.com
Re-founded 100 years after Tennessee state prohibition shut them down in 1909, they are looking for property to build their distillery. In the mean time they are having their Belle Meade Bourbon, which is a small batch sour mash straight whiskey with high rye content, distilled for them through a contract distillery.

OLE SMOKY DISTILLERY
903 Parkway #128
Gatlinburg, TN 37738
Tel: (865) 436-6995
Email: shine@osdistillery.com
www.olesmokymoonshine.com
They produce Ole Smoky Original Moonshine, which is an unaged corn whiskey made from a mash bill of 80% corn (locally sourced from farmers in East Tennessee) and 20% other grains and or sugar. Their moonshine is also the base of a wide variety of fruit flavored spirits. They also produce Ole Smoky White Lightnin', which is made from 100% re-distilled neutral grain spirits.

Pinckney Bend Distillery | Missouri

Pinckney Bend distillery They are currently aging Pinckney Bend Whiskey. [page 101]

POPCORN SUTTON DISTILLING
PO Box 90371
Nashville TN 37209
Email: info@popcornsuttonswhiskey.com
www.popcornsuttonswhiskey.com
Apprentice turn distiller Jamey Grosser, is producing Popcorn Sutton's Tennessee White Whiskey in honor of the long time moonshiner.

PRICHARDS DISTILLERY
11 Kelso Smithland Rd.
Kelso, TN 37348
Tel: (931) 433 5454
Email: info@prichardsdistillery.com
www.prichardsdistillery.com
Opened in 1997, they make Benjamin Prichard's Tennessee Whiskey, Single Malt Whiskey, Double Barreled Bourbon, Rye Whiskey, un-aged Lincoln County Lightning and two whiskey liqueurs.

SHORT MOUNTAIN DISTILLERY
119 Mountain Spirits
Woodbury, TN 37190
Tel: (615) 216-0830
Email: info@shortmountaindistillery.com
www.shortmountaindistillery.com
Founded in 2010, they produce small-batch, Tennessee Moonshine, Bourbon and Tennessee Whiskey from corn grown and stone-milled in Cannon County, Tennessee.

SPEAKEASY SPIRITS
900 44th Ave. North, Suite 100
Nashville, TN 37209
Tel: (615) 569-1968
Email: jenny@speakeasymarketing.com
www.speakeasy-spirits.com
Founded in 2009, they produce a Tennessee Whiskey Cream Liqueur called Whisper Creek Tennessee Sipping Cream.

TENNESSEE DISTILLING COMPANY
900 44th Ave. North #500
Nashville, TN 37209
Tel: (615) 244-7856
Email: info@collierandmckeel.com
www.collierandmckeel.com
Founded in 2010, they produce three whiskey products: Collier and McKeel Charcoal Mellowed White Dog Whiskey, which is made from a mash bill of corn, rye and malted barley, filtered through sugar maple charcoal and bottled at 100 proof. Their Handcrafted Sour Mash Whiskey takes the same mash bill, ages it in very small oak barrels after filtering and is bottled at 43% abv.

TENNESSEE SPIRITS COMPANY
PO Box 71
One Whiskey Way
Pulaski, TN 38478
Tel: (888) 784-2946
Email: Built into their website
www.tennesseespiritscompany.com
Founded in 2011, they are currently building a distillery with an annual production capacity of 5 million cases. In the mean time they are bottling three products from whiskey they purchased in Lincoln County.

TENN SOUTH DISTILLERY
3979 Albert Mattews Rd.
Columbia, TN 38401
Tel: (931) 215-4736
Email: blair@tennsouthdistillery.com
www.balconesdistilling.com
They broke ground in May 2012 and plan to produce white spirits and Tennessee Whiskey. The Tennessee Whiskey will be made from a mash bill of corn, malted barley, wheat and rye, charcoal mellowed and aged between 2 and 5 years in new charred American white oak.

TEXAS

BALCONES DISTILLERY
212 South 17th St.
Waco, TX 76707
Tel: (254) 755-6003
Email: Built into their website
www.balconesdistillery.com
Products include Baby Blue Whisky, made from blue corn, as well as a peated and non-peated version of Balcones Single Malt Whisky.

BONE SPIRITS LLC
802 North East 1st St.
Smithville, TX 78957
Tel: (512) 237-5000
Email: info@bonespirits.com
www.bonespirits.com
Founded in 2010, they produce two versions of their 100% corn whiskey: Fitch's Goat Moonshine, bottled at 87% proof and Fitch's Goat Whiskey which has been aged and bottled at 97 proof.

Headframe Spirits | Montana

Headframe Spirits They produce two whiskeys: Neversweat Bourbon Whiskey and Destroying Angel Whiskey which are both named after mining sites in Butte. [page 101]

FIRESTONE & ROBERTSON DISTILLING COMPANY
901 West Vickery Boulevard
Fort Worth, TX 76104
Tel: (817) 840-9140
Email: info@frdistilling.com
www.frdistilling.com
They currently sell TX Blended Whiskey while their F&R Straight Bourbon Whisky matures for a full two years. The bourbon should be ready some time in 2014.

GARRISON BROTHERS DISTILLERY
1827 Hye-Albert Rd.
Hye, TX 78635
Tel: (830) 392-0246
Email: dan@garrisonbros.com
www.garrisonbros.com
This Texas distillery produces a number of vintage whiskeys that change in their mash bill, types of barrels used and length of maturation. They have released a couple of bourbons so far and are working on a white corn whiskey, rye, a cask strength and a five plus years old reserve whiskey.

POWDERFINGER SPIRITS LLC
4568 Dacy Lane Building 2
Buda, TX 78610
Tel: (718) 219-6850
Email: inquiries@powderfingerspirits.com
www.powderfingerspirits.com
Founded in 2011, they are producing Bourbon whiskey in small batches using locally sourced ingredients, and aging it for four years in new charred American Oak barrels.

QUENTIN D. WITHERSPOON DISTILLERY
545 N Cowan Ave Suite F
Lewisville, TX 75057
Tel: (214) 418-1959
Email: witherspoon_q@yahoo.com
While they are currently under construction they have plans to produce a couple of different whiskeys. Their 1836 Whiskey will be a Tennessee style whiskey with a mash bill of corn, barley and rye that commemorates the founding of the State of Texas. They also plan to produce Cross Timbers Single Malt Whiskey, which will be made from lightly mesquite smoked malted barley and aged in ex-bourbon barrels.

RANGER CREEK BREWING & DISTILLERY
4834 Whirlwind Dr. #102
San Antonio, TX 78217
Tel: (210) 775-2099
Email: info@drinkrangercreek.com
www.drinkrangercreek.com
Founded in 2010, this brewery and distillery produces Ranger Creek 36 Texas Bourbon Whiskey, which was aged in small oak barrels and Texas Straight Bourbon Whiskey which is maturing for at least two years before bottling.

REBECCA CREEK DISTILLERY
26605 Bulverde Rd., Bldg. B
San Antonio, TX 78260
Tel: 830-714-4581
Email: info@rebeccacreekdistillery.com
www.rebeccacreekdistillery.com
They produce Rebecca Creek Fine Texas Spirit Whiskey.

YELLOW ROSE DISTILLING
34444 Wright Rd.
Pinehurst, TX 77362
Email: sales@yellowrosedistilling.com
www.yellowrosedistilling.com
They produce Yellow Rose Outlaw Bourbon which, is made from 100% organic Texas grown corn and aged in new charred American Oak. They are also aging a single malt whiskey that will bottled at a future date.

UTAH

HIGH WEST DISTILLERY
703 Park Ave.
Park City, UT 84060
Tel: (801) 972 2566
Email: info@highwestdistillery.com
www.highwestdistillery.com
High West Distillery produces a wide range of whiskeys including High West Rendezvous Rye Whiskey; Double Rye; and Campfire, a blend of bourbon, rye and scotch whiskeys.

VERMONT

APPALACHIAN GAP DISTILLERY
88 Maineli Rd.
Middlebury, VT 05753
Tel: (802) 877-1577
Email: info@appgap.com
www.appalachiangap.com
While they are currently under construction they have plans to begin producing whiskey and other spirits.

CALEDONIA SPIRITS
46 Buffalo Mountain Commons Dr.
Hardwick, VT 05843
Tel: (802) 472-8000
Email: info@caledoniaspirits.com
caledoniaspirits.com
Besides vodka and gin they are also making a whiskey from Vermont grown grains.

GOAMERICAGO BEVERAGES LLC
Mailing Address:
1030 Palmer Rd.
Shoreham, VT 05770
Physical Address:
2139 Quiet Valley Rd.
Shoreham, VT 05770
Tel: (802) 385-1093 / (802) 385-1046 / (802) 897-7700
Email: info@whistlepigfarm.com
www.whistlepigwhiskey.com
Founded in 2006, they bottle WhistlePig Straight Rye Whiskey which they currently source from Canada. Their ultimate goal is to operate as a farm distillery where they will grow and distill their own rye.

SMUGGLERS' NOTCH DISTILLERY
276 Main St.
Jeffersonville, VT 05464
Tel: (802) 309-3077
Email: Built into their website
www.smugglersnotchdistillery.com
Along with their vodka, gin and rum they are planning to produce Smugglers' Notch Whiskey. They distilled their spirit from a mash of about 80% corn and 20% wheat. They are also using a proprietary method of maturing their spirit in charred white oak barrels.

VIRGINIA

CATOCTIN CREEK DISTILLING COMPANY
37251 C East Richardson Lane
Purcellville, VA 20132-3505
Tel: (540) 751-8407
Email: info@catoctincreek.com
www.catoctincreekdistilling.com
Founded in 2009, they produce Roundstone Rye which they make from 100% organic rye grain and age in new Minnesota white oak barrels. They also produce an unaged version called Mosby's Spirit. Both are certified organic and kosher.

COPPER FOX
9 River Lane
Sperryville, VA 22740
Tel: (540) 987 8554
Email: rw@copperfox.biz
www.copperfox.biz
Founded in 2000 they produce Wasmund's Single Malt Whiskey, Copper Fox Rye Whiskey, as well as the un-aged Wasmund's Single Malt Spirit and Wasmund's Rye Spirit. They are also working on a Bourbon that is not ready to be bottled.

GEORGE WASHINGTON DISTILLERY
Mount Vernon Memorial Highway
Mount Vernon, VA 22309
Tel: (703) 780-2000
Email: jstrong@mountvernon.org
www.discus.org/heritage/washington.asp
They produce a very limited amount of an aged and unaged rye whiskey based on George Washington's original mash bill of 60% rye, 35% corn, 5% barley. The designs for the stills and floor plans for the distillery were reconstructed from archeological and historical records and rebuilt at the original location.

RESERVOIR DISTILLERY
1800 A Summit Ave.
Richmond, VA 23230
Tel: (804) 921-2621
Email: info@reservoirdistillery.com
www.reservoirdistillery.com
Founded in 2008, they produce Reservoir Bourbon, Rye and Wheat Whiskeys.

STILLHOUSE DISTILLERY
Belmont Farms
13490 Cedar Run Rd.
Culpepper, VA 22701
Tel: (540) 825 3207
Email: info@virginiamoonshine.com
www.virginiamoonshine.com
www.virginiawhiskey.com
This farm distillery produces The Original Moonshine Clear Corn Whiskey, which is 100% corn whiskey made entirely from corn grown on the farm. They also produce Kopper Kettle Virginia Whiskey, which is made from a mash bill of corn, wheat and barley, presoaked with oak and apple wood chips and aged for two years in oak barrels.

VIRGILINA DISTILLING COMPANY
1141 7th St.
Virgilina, VA 24598
Tel: (434) 579-2460
Email: swburkholder@gmail.com
Their farm grows Heirloom Hickory King White Corn and when production begins they will start with unaged corn whiskey bottled at 90 proof and flavored corn whiskeys such as peach and apple. Eventually they are planning to produce bourbon, and seasonal runs of eau-de-vie and brandy. Their aged spirits will mature in new charred oak barrels but they are also thinking of experimenting with used wine barrels in which to age their corn whiskeys.

VIRGINIA DISTILLERY COMPANY
299 Eades Lane
Box 509
Lovingston, VA 22949
Tel: (434) 325-1299
Email: info@vadistillery.com
www.vadistillery.com
While their distillery is under construction they are selling Eades Double Malt Whiskies which are each blends of two malt whiskies from single regions of Scotland. Eventually they plan to produce Virginia Single Malt Whiskey, which will be double distilled on a large Scottish-made copper pot stills and aged for at least 3 years in ex-bourbon barrels.

WASHINGTON

2 BAR SPIRITS
2960 4th Ave. South, Suite 106
Seattle, WA 98134
Email: info@2barspirits.com
www.2barspirits.com
Along with vodka they currently produce 2bar Moonshine. They also plan to release an aged whiskey.

5 O'CLOCK DISTILLERY
101 Maple St.
Cashmere, WA 98815
Tel: (509) 860-0102
Email: 5oclock@5oclocksomewheredistillery.com
www.5oclockdistillery.com
They produce three whiskey products: Moonshine, made from 100% corn and distilled only once; Sunshine, which is an aged version of their corn whiskey; and Wheat Whiskey, which is made from 100% Washington wheat and aged in charred oak barrels.

BAINBRIDGE ORGANIC DISTILLERS
9727 Coppertop Loop NE
Bainbridge Island, WA 98110
Tel: (206) 842-3184
Email: info@bainbridgedistillers.com
www.bainbridgedistillers.com
Along with Vodka and Gin they also produce Bainbridge Battle Point Whiskey, which is a wheat whiskey that they make from organic wheat and age in 10-gallon American oak barrels for 12 to 18 months.

BATCH 206 DISTILLERY
1417 Elliott Ave. West
Seattle, WA 98199
Tel: (206) 863-8777
Email: jeff@batch206.com
www.batch206.com
Besides vodka and gin they are also producing: Gold Buckle Club Malt Whiskey, which they make from 85% two-row pale ale malted barley, and a variety of other malts including caramel, crystal, and chocolate; Ballard Bourbon, which beside corn includes rye, malted wheat and malted barley; Their Alki Rye Whiskey, is made with rye, corn, malted wheat and malted barley. All of their whiskeys are aged for 24 months in 225-liter American oak barrels.

BELLEWOOD DISTILLING
231 Ten Mile Rd.
Lynden, WA 98264-9634
Tel: (360) 398-9187
Email: Built into their website
www.bellewoodfarms.com
While they are currently under construction, they plan to produce whiskey and a variety of other spirits.

BLACK HERON SPIRITS
8011 Keen Rd.
Box 4535
West Richland, WA 99353
Tel: (509) 643-2295
Email: Joel@blackheronspirits.com
www.blackheronspirits.com
Among other spirits they also produce an aged and unaged version of Desert Lightning corn whiskey. The aged version spent 10 months in used charred white oak barrels before bottling.

COPPERWORKS DISTILLING
51 University St.
Seattle, WA 98101
Tel: (206) 920-5142
Email: jason@copperworksdistilling.com
www.copperworksdistilling.com
Currently under construction, they eventually plan to produce whiskey and gin.

DRY COUNTY DISTILLERY
521 Delta Ave.
Marysville, WA 98270
Tel: (425) 343-8021
Email: DryCountyDistillery@msn.com, info@drycountydistillery.com
www.drycountydistillery.com
Along with brandy gin and vodka, this family operated distillery has also produced a limited amount of whisky. Their whiskey was made from barley, oats, rye and other grains. As of June 2013 their un-aged whiskey bottled at 125 proof was nearly sold out and they plan to release a bottling at 80 proof.

DRY FLY DISTILLING
1003 East Trent #200
Spokane, WA 99202
Tel: (509) 489-2112
Email: don@dryflydistilling.com
www.dryflydistilling.com
They produce Dry Fly Washington Bourbon, which is bottled at 101 proof. They also produce Dry Fly Washington Wheat Whiskey. Both are made from locally sourced grains like wheat, barley, triticale (a durum wheat rye hybrid), oats, corn, malted wheat, malted barley and each whiskey is aged for at least 2 years before bottling.

EZRA COX DISTILLERY
719 North Tower Ave.
Centralia, WA 98531
Email: ezracoxiii@gmail.com
While they are waiting for their label approval they are producing a moonshine they described as an unaged single malt whiskey, made from 100% Washington grown malted barley.

FREMONT MISCHIEF DISTILLERY
132 North Canal St.
Seattle, WA 98103
Tel: (206) 547-0838
Email: info@fremontmischief.com
www.fremontmischief.com
They produce two whiskeys: John Jacob 100% rye grain whiskey; Fremont Mischief Whiskey, which is an 8-year old rye whiskey.

GNOSTALGIC SPIRITS DISTILLERY
920 South Holgate St.
Seattle, WA 98134
Tel: (206) 267-8626
Email: contact@gnostalgicspirits.com
www.gnostalgicspirits.com
While currently producing an absinth they are planning to use Washington grown wheat, corn, barley and rye to produce a whiskey.

GOLDEN DISTILLERY
9746 Samish Island Rd.
Bow, WA 98232
Tel: (360) 542-8332
Email: goldenartisanspirits@gmail.com
www.goldendistillery.com
They produce two whiskeys. Samish Bay Whiskey, is a single malt whiskey which is also released in Reserve edition, and White Gold Whiskey.

HARDWARE DISTILLERY
24210 North Hwy. 101
P.O. Box 129
Hoodsport, WA 98548
Tel: (206) 300-0877
Email: Built into their website
www.thehardwaredistillery.com
This new distillery plans to produce a whiskey that displays the character of the Pacific Northwest. It will be aged in oak barrels and exposed to the salt air of the Hood Canal.

HERITAGE DISTILLING
3207 57th Court Northwest
Gig Harbor, WA 98335
Tel: (253) 509-0008
Email: info@heritagedistilling.com
www.heritagedistilling.com
Founded and operated by Jennifer and Justin Steifel, they produce Elk Rider™ Whiskey, Wherskey™ Light Whiskey and Washington's Rye Whiskey™. They are a Field to Flask™ distillery that sources their grain from local Washington state farmers, mills, mashes, ferments, distills and bottles their spirits. They also like to trademark things.

JP TRODDEN DISTILLING
18646 142nd Ave. NE
Woodinville, WA 98072
Tel: (206) 339-6291
Email: mark@jptroddendistilling.com
They began producing whiskey in May 2011 and their Small Batch Bourbon should be ready for release in Fall 2013.

MAC DONALD DISTILLERIES
104 Ave. C
Snohomish, WA 98290
Tel: (425) 275-1328
Email: yeuriza@yahoo.com
www.macdonalddistillery.com
They produce Ty Wolfe Whiskey

OOLA DISTILLERY
1413 East Union St.
Seattle, WA 98122 Tel: (360) 589-1829
Email: info@ooladistillery.com www.ooladistillery.com
This new distillery is beginning production of their White Whiskey and Waitsburg Whiskey.

PROJECT V DISTILLERY & SAUSAGE COMPANY
19495 144th Ave. NE
#A-130
Woodinville, WA 98072
Tel: (425) 398-1738
Email: projectvdistillery@gmail.com
www.projectvdistillery.com
Along with their vodka they are also making a white winter wheat whiskey that is aged for 2+ years in charred oak barrels.

SKIP ROCK DISTILLERS
104 Ave. C
Snohomish, WA 98290
Tel: (425) 330-4885
Email: info@skiprockdistillers.com
www.skiprockdistillers.com
Founded in 2009, they are producing Headwaters Whiskey, which is a multi-grain unaged spirit.

WESTLAND DISTILLERY
9320 15th Ave. So. # CE-2
Seattle, WA 93108
Tel: (206) 767-7250
Email: info@westlanddistillery.com
www.westlanddistillery.com
While they are currently under construction they plan to produce an American Single Malt Whiskey.

WHIDBEY ISLAND DISTILLERY
3466 Craw Road
Langley, WA 98260
Tel: (360) 321-4715
Email: hello@whidbeydistillery.com
www.whidbeydistillery.com
They plan to produce a Rye Whiskey.

WISHKAH RIVER DISTILLERY
2210 Port Industrial Rd.
Box 415
Aberdeen, WA 98520-0098
Tel: (360) 589-1829
Email: sue@wishkahriver.com
www.wishkahriver.com
Among a wide variety of spirits they also have plans to produce whiskey as well.

WOODINVILLE WHISKEY COMPANY
16110 Woodinville Redmond Rd. NE, Ste. 3
Woodinville, WA 98072
Tel: (425) 486-1199
Email: info@woodinvillewhiskeyco.com
www.woodinvillewhiskeyco.com
They produce Headlong White Dog Whiskey, which they make from their bourbon recipe of corn, wheat and barley. They also produce two aged whiskies that they mature in small barrels called Mashbill No. 9 Bourbon Whiskey and 100% Rye Whiskey.

WEST VIRGINIA

ISAIAH MORGAN DISTILLERY
45 Winery Lane
Summersville, WV 26651
Tel: (304) 872 7332
Email: isiah@kuinet.com
www.kirkwood-wine.com
The Isaiah Morgan Distillery's two whiskey products include Isaiah Morgan Rye Whiskey and Southern Moon Corn Liquor.

PINCHGUT HOLLOW DISTILLERY
1602 Tulip Lane
Fairmount, WV 26554
Tel: (304) 534-2516
Email: Built into their website
www.hestonfarm.com
They produce two whiskeys: Buckwheat Moon, they made from 51% buckwheat, 34% corn, 15% barley grown on their farm and barrel aged for 30 days before being bottled at 100 proof; Their Corn Shine is 100% corn whiskey also barrel-aged for 30 days and bottled at 100 proof.

Hillrock Distillery & Malt House | New York

Hillrock Distillery & Malt House Distillation at the estate commenced in October 2011 and they have released the Hillrock Solera Aged Bourbon Whiskey. Besides corn the mash bill is about 37% rye, and the bourbon has an average age of 6 years before being bottled at 46.3% abv. They are in the process of ageing the soon to be released Estate Single Malt and Estate Rye whiskeys which will be made from organic barley and rye grown and malted at the Hillrock Estate. [page 104]

SMOOTH AMBLER SPIRITS COMPANY
PO Box 133,
745 Industrial Park Rd.
Maxwelton, WV 24957
Tel: (304) 497-3123
Email: jlittle@smoothambler.com
www.smoothambler.com

Founded in 2009, They are producing Yearling Bourbon Whiskey, which they make from a mash bill of corn, wheat, barley, aged in small casks for about 18 months and bottled at 92 proof. They also produce an unaged version called Exceptional White Whiskey that is bottled at 100 proof.

WEST VIRGINIA DISTILLING COMPANY
1425 Saratoga Ave., Suite G
Morgantown, WV 26505
Tel: (304) 599-0960
Email: pfireman@verizon.net
www.mountainmoonshine.com

West Virginia Distilling produces Mountain Moonshine West Virginia Spirit Whiskey in both 80 and 100 proof versions.

WISCONSIN

45TH PARALLEL SPIRITS
1570 Madison Ave.
New Richmond, WI 45107
Tel: (715) 246-0565
Email: info@45thparallelspirits.com
www.45thparallelspirits.com

While whiskey production began in 2009, much of it went to contracts. They have released Border Bourbon, and they also plan to produce a rye and wheat whiskey. Each will be a straight whiskey, aged between 2 and 3 years in 53-gallon oak casks. Some of the whiskey will continue to age for a few more years for a 4 year release. All their corn, rye and wheat is sourced from a local farm and the spent grain is used as cattle feed.

AEPPELTREOW WINERY & DISTILLERY
1072 288th Avenue
Burlington, WI 53105
Tel: (262) 878-5345
Email: cider@appletrue.com
www.aeppeltreow.com

Among a wide variety of products they also produce Brown Dog Whiskey which they make from locally grown sweet sorghum. The whiskey is aged in ex-apple brandy barrels for one or two months and then stored in stainless steel for a month with a combination of seasoned, toasted and charred, oak, cherry wood, apple wood, and chestnut wood chips.

DEATH'S DOOR SPIRITS
2220 Eagle Dr.
Middletown, WI 53562
Tel: (608) 831-1083
Email: info@deathsdoorspirits.com
deathsdoorspirits.com

Along with vodka and gin they produce Death's Door White Whisky, which they make from 80% organic Washington Island Wheat and 20% organic malted barley from Chilton, Wisconsin.

GREAT LAKES DISTILLERY
616 West Virginia St.
Milwaukee, WI 53204
Tel: (414) 431-8683
Email: info@greatlakesdistillery.com
greatlakesdistillery.com

Among other spirits they also produce Kinnickinnic Whiskey which is a blend of their own malt whiskey with straight bourbon from another distillery. It is unfiltered and bottled at 86 proof.

LO ARTISAN DISTILLERY
1607 South Stevenson Pier Rd.
Sturgeon Bay, WI 54235
Tel: (337) 660-1600
Email: poclo@lo-artisandistillery.com
lo-artisandistillery.com

This family distillery produces a traditional Hmong rice spirit called Yerlo which they bottle at 120 proof. White not technically a whiskey because they do not age it in oak, it is similar in some respects to American moonshine.

OLD SUGAR DISTILLERY
931 East Main St. #8
Madison, WI 53703
Tel: (608) 260-0812
Email: madisondistillery@gmail.com
www.madisondistillery.com

Among a variety of liqueurs they also produce Queen Jennie Sorghum Whiskey, which they make from 100% Wisconsin grown sorghum and age in small charred oak barrels from Minnesota.

YAHARA BAY DISTILLERS
3118 Kingsley Way,
Madison, WI 53713
Tel: (608) 275-1050
Email: Built into their website
www.yaharabay.com

Among a diverse product line they produce Yahara Bay Whiskey which is distilled from a four grain mash bill of corn, wheat, barley and rye all grown in Wisconsin. They also produce and unaged version called Yahara Bay Lightning which is bottled from the still at 110 proof.

Panther Distillery | Minnesota

Panther Distillery Currently they produce White Water Whiskey which is made from a bourbon whisky mash of locally gown corn and red wheat. They also have three whiskeys maturing with a planed release in 2014. Their Ironwood Whiskey is made from Minnesota red wheat and yellow corn. Their Red Rye Whiskey is made from 100% locally gown rye and aged in charred oak barrels. Their Blue Earth Bourbon is made from the same grain bill as their White Water Whiskey. [page 99]

WYOMING

RANGE & RIVER DISTILLING
63 Sage Creek Rd.
Cody, WY 82414
Tel: (307) 761-1380
Email: trinakedspur@yahoo.com
www.rangeandriverdistilling.com
www.singletrackspirits.com

This one man distillery is currently working on a wheat whiskey that he makes from 92% hard red winter wheat and 8% 6-row barley, both grown locally in northern Wyoming and southern Montana. The distiller is aging the whiskey in large oak casks and keeping watch for when they are ready.

WYOMING WHISKEY
100 South Nelson
Kirby, Wyoming 82430
Tel: (917) 902 6217
Email: donna@wyomingwhiskey.com

They began bourbon production on July 4, 2009. Their first public offering was slated for release in December 2012.

LATIN AMERICA

Union Distillery | Brazil

Union Distillery Located in Veranópolis, among the mountains of southern Brazil, Union Distillery believes its mild climate and abundance of cold fresh water makes it ideally situated for whisky production. [page 127]

BRAZIL

DESTILARIAS BUSNELLO
St. Francisco Ferrari, 765 Quarter Barracão
Post Office Box: 56 95700-000
Bento Gonçalves, Rio Grande do Sul
Brazil
Tel: +55 (54) 3452 1719
Email: administrativo@destilariabusnello.com.br
www.destilariabusnello.com.br/eng/index.html
Busnello Distillery makes Pitt's Blended Whisky which is aged for 8 years in oak barrels.

DESTILARIAS REUNIDAS LENZI LTDA
Coronel Vinancio Ferreira Alves Adorno, 89
5 Andar, 13800-000
Mogi Mirim, Sao Paulo
Brazil
Tel: +55 019 3806 9208
They make a whisky called The Personal Blend.

HUEBLEIN DO BRASIL COM IND
Rue Arapore, 655
Sorocaba, 05608-001
Sao Paulo
Brazil
Tel: +55 11 816 8619
Email: info@campari.com
Currently owned by Campari, they produce several blends like Old Eight Blended Whisky, and they also make Durfee Hall Single Malt Whisky.

UNION DISTILLERY MALTWHISKY DO BRASIL
Matriz-Veranopolis
Av. Julio de Oliveira, 312-Cx. P. 110
Veranopolis, Rio Grande do Sul
Brazil
Tel: +55 54 3441 1366
Email: maltwhisky@maltwhisky.com.br
www.maltwhisky.com.br
Founded in 1948, this cachaça distillery began making malt whisky in 1972 and selling it in bulk to other beverage companies. While they continue to sell the majority of their production to blenders, in 2008 they began selling Union Club Whisky which is aged for 5 years in ex-bourbon barrels and bottled a 38% abv.

VINICOLA CORDELIER LTDA
Rodovia RST 470 km 219, 75
Caixa Postal 721, CEP 95700-000
Bento Gonçalves, Rio Grande do Sul
Brazil
Vinicola, makes mostly wines and cachaça, but also produces several blended whiskies, such as Malt Barrilete Blended and O Monge Blended Whiskey.

MEXICO

D.M. DISTILLERY CO. S.A.
Av. Francisco Villa, No.103 Norte. Centro 32000
Ciudad Juarez, Chihuahua
Mexico
Tel: +52 (656) 612-3278
The only whiskey distillery in Mexico currently produces Golden CAP Whiskey, Juarez Whiskey Straight American, and Juarez Whiskey Straight American Bourbon.

URUGUAY

COMPANIA ANCAP DE BEBIDAS Y ALCOHOLES S.A.
Rambla Baltasar Brum
Montevideo
Uruguay
Tel: 598 2306 1747
Email: caba@caba.com.uy
www.caba.com.uy
This distillery in Uruguay produces several blends, including Golden King Blended, Mac Pay 6-Year Old Blended, and Whiskey Anejo.

VENEZUELA

DESTILARIA CARUPANO
Hacienda Altamira, Macarapana
Carupano
Venezuela
Tel: +58 (294) 331 13 85
Email: info@roncarupano.com
roncarupano.com
Carupano mostly produces distilled spirits from sugar cane products. Their Scotty's Dry Spirit Liquor is a blend of Scottish whisky and distilled sugar cane.

ADDITIONAL SOURCES

Alaska Alcohol Beverage Control Board. "Master List of All Current Licenses." Accessed June 9, 2012. HYPERLINK "http://commerce.alaska.gov/dnn/Portals/9/pub/ MasterList.xls.xls" http://commerce.alaska.gov/dnn/Portals/9/pub/ MasterList.xls.xls.

Alternative Whisky Academy. "Whisky Distilleries, Producers and Distributors." Accessed May 22, 2012. HYPERLINK "http://www.awa.dk/whisky/stills/index.htm" http://www.awa.dk/whisky/stills/index.htm.

American Distilling Institute. 2012 Distillers Resource Directory. California: American Distilling Institute, 2012.

Arizona Department of Liquor Licenses and Control. "License Master Table." Accessed June 9, 2012. HYPERLINK "http://www.azliquor.gov/query/master.csv" http://www.azliquor.gov/query/master.csv.

California Department of Alcoholic Beverage Control. "License Query System." Accessed June 18, 2012. HYPERLINK "http://www.abc.ca.gov/datport/LQSMenu.html" http://www.abc.ca.gov/datport/LQSMenu.html.

Colorado Department of Revenue Liquor and Tobacco Enforcement Division. "All State Liquor Licenses." Accessed July 8, 2012. HYPERLINK "http://www.colorado.gov/cs/Satellite?c= Page&childpagename=Rev-Liquor%2FLIQLayout&cid=1209635770580& pagename=LIQWrapper" http://www.colorado.gov/cs/Satellite?c= Page&childpagename=Rev-Liquor%2FLIQLayout&cid=1209635770580& pagename=LIQWrapper.

Comptroller of Maryland Regulatory & Enforcement Division. "Alcohol and Tobacco Tax Licenses and Permits." Accessed July 16, 2012. HYPERLINK "https://interactive.marylandtaxes.com/webapps/licprt/" https://interactive.marylandtaxes.com/webapps/licprt/

Connecticut eLicensing Website. "Available Rosters for Download." Accessed June 22, 2012. HYPERLINK "https://www.elicense.ct.gov/Lookup/GenerateRoster.aspx" https://www.elicense.ct.gov/Lookup/GenerateRoster.aspx.

Florida Department of Business & Professional Regulation. "Alcoholic Beverage and Tabacco Public Records." Accessed June 20, 2012. HYPERLINK "http://www.myfloridalicense.com/dbpr/sto/file_download/public-records-ABT.html" http://www.myfloridalicense.com /dbpr/sto/file_download/public-records-ABT.html.

Indiana Alcohol and Tobacco Commission. "accessIndiana Business Permits." Accessed July 9, 2012. HYPERLINK "http://www.in.gov/apps/atc/permit/search/navigation.action?location1= Business+Permits" http://www.in.gov/apps/atc/permit/search/navigation.action?location1= Business+Permits

Kansas Department of Revenue. "Liquor Licensee Search." Accessed July 12, 2012. HYPERLINK "https://www.kdor.org/abc/licensee/Search.aspx" https://www.kdor.org/abc/licensee/Search.aspx.

Louisiana Alcohol & Tobacco Control. "Available Rosters for Download." Accessed July 13, 2012. HYPERLINK "http://atcpub.license.louisiana.gov/Lookup/GenerateRoster.aspx" http://atcpub.license.louisiana.gov/Lookup/GenerateRoster.aspx.

Maine Department of Public Safety Liquor Licensing & Compliance. "Current Active Liquor Licenses." Accessed July 14, 2012. HYPERLINK "http://www.maine.gov/dps/liqr/active_ licenses.htm" http://www.maine.gov/dps/liqr/active_ licenses.htm.

Malt Maddness. "Distillery Data." Accessed May 26, 2012. HYPERLINK "http://www.maltmadness.com/whisky/" http://www.maltmadness.com/whisky/.

Michigan Department of Licensing and Regulatory Affairs Liquor Control Commission. "Manufactures and Wholesalers List by Type." Accessed July 18, 2012. http://www.michigan.gov/documents/dleg/MW_NameAddress_5-2010_321616_7.pdf.

Minnesota Department of Public Saftey Alcohol & Gambling Enforcement Division. "Liquor License Information." Accessed July 17, 2012. HYPERLINK "https://app.dps.mn.gov/age/" https://app.dps.mn.gov/age/.

Nebraska Liquor Control Commission. "Licensee Search." Accessed July 19, 2012. HYPERLINK "http://www.lcc.ne.gov/license_search/licsearch.cgi" http://www.lcc.ne.gov/license_search/licsearch.cgi.

New Hampshire Online Licensing. "Facility Search." Accessed July 20, 2012. HYPERLINK "https://nhlicenses.nh.gov/MyLicense%20Verification/Search.aspx?facility=Y" https://nhlicenses.nh.gov/MyLicense%20Verification/Search.aspx?facility=Y.

New Mexico Regulation & Licensing Department. "Facility Search." Accessed June 10, 2012. HYPERLINK "http://rldverification.rld.state.nm.us/Verification/Search.aspx?facility=Y" http://rldverification.rld.state.nm.us/Verification/Search.aspx?facility=Y.

New York State Liquor Authority. "Liquor Distillers in New York State." Division of Alcoholic Beverage Control. June 11, 2012.

North Dakota Office of State Tax Commissioner. "Alcohol License and Permit List." Accessed June 7, 2012. HYPERLINK "http://www.nd.gov/tax/alcohol/forms/web-licenseandpermitlist.xls" http://www.nd.gov/tax/alcohol/forms/web-licenseandpermitlist.xls.

Ohio Department of Commerce Division of Liquor Control. "Web Database Search." Accessed June 9, 2012. HYPERLINK "https://www.comapps.ohio.gov/liqr/liqr_apps/PermitLookup/PermitHolder.aspx" https://www.comapps.ohio.gov/liqr/liqr_apps/PermitLookup/PermitHolder.aspx.

Oregon Liquor Control Commission. "Current Licenses – All Businesses." Accessed June 13, 2012. HYPERLINK "http://www.olcc.state.or.us/pdfs/licenses_by_type_excel.xls" http://www.olcc.state.or.us/pdfs/licenses_by_type_excel.xls.

Pennsylvania Liquor Control Board. "PLCB License Search System." Accessed July 21, 2012. HYPERLINK "http://www.lcbapps.lcb.state.pa.us/webapp/Agency/SearchCenter/Public LicenseeSearchDefault.asp" http://www.lcbapps.lcb.state.pa.us/webapp/Agency/SearchCenter/Public LicenseeSearchDefault.asp.

Planet Whiskies. "World Distilleries." Accessed May 20, 2012. HYPERLINK "http://www.planetwhiskies.com/distilleries.html" http://www.planetwhiskies.com/distilleries.html.

ScotchWhisky.net "Whisky Distilleries." Accessed May 22, 2012. HYPERLINK "http://www.scotchwhisky.net/distilleries/index.php" http://www.scotchwhisky.net/distilleries/index.php.

ScotlandWhisky. "Distilleries." Accessed May 21, 2012. HYPERLINK "http://www.scotlandwhisky.com/ distilleries/#" http://www.scotlandwhisky.com/ distilleries/#.

State of Illinois Liquor Control Commission. "License Search Options." Accessed July 10, 2012. HYPERLINK "http://www.state.il.us/lcc/tdq.asp" http://www.state.il.us/lcc/tdq.asp.

State of Iowa Alcohol Beverages Division. "License Search." Accessed July 11, 2012. HYPERLINK "https://elicensing.iowaabd.com/LicenseSearch.aspx" https://elicensing.iowaabd.com/LicenseSearch.aspx.

Texas Alcoholic Beverage Commission. "Public Inquiry System." Accessed July 21, 2012. HYPERLINK "http://www.tabc.state.tx.us/PublicInquiry/Roster.aspx" http://www.tabc.state.tx.us/PublicInquiry/Roster.aspx.

Vermont Department of Liquor Control. "Distilled Spirits Manufactures." Accessed July 23, 2012. HYPERLINK "http://liquorcontrol.vermont.gov/download/distillers.txt" http://liquorcontrol.vermont.gov/download/distillers.txt.

Virginia Department of Alcoholic Beverage Control. "Licensee Search Form." Accessed July 24, 2012. HYPERLINK "http://www.abc.state.va.us/licenseeSearch/jsp/controller.jsp" http://www.abc.state.va.us/licenseeSearch/jsp/controller.jsp.

Washington State Liquor Control Board. "Craft Distillers List." Accessed July 25, 2012. HYPERLINK "http://liq.wa.gov/publications/Public_Records/2012-Craft-Distilleries/Craft%20 Distillery%20List%20July%202012.xlsx" http://liq.wa.gov/publications/Public_Records/2012-Craft-Distilleries/Craft%20 Distillery%20List%20July%202012.xlsx.

West Virginia Alcohol Beverage Control Administration. "License Search." Accessed July 26, 2012. HYPERLINK "https://apps.wv.gov/ABCA/LicenseSearch/Forms/" https://apps.wv.gov/ABCA/LicenseSearch/Forms/.

Whiskey Portal. "Whiskey Regions." Accessed May 25, 2012. HYPERLINK "http://www.whiskyportal.com/ region_overview.asp" http://www.whiskyportal.com/ region_overview.asp.

Whisky. "Complete Guide to Scotch Whisky." Accessed May 23, 2012. HYPERLINK "http://www.whisky.com/" http://www.whisky.com/.

A. Smith Bowman | Virginia

A. Smith Bowman Owned by Sazerac, A. Smith Bowman produces Virginia Gentleman Straight Bourbon and Virginia Gentleman 90 Proof Small Batch Bourbon.

Appendices

Distilleries Operated by Major Conglomerates

BACARDI

Founded in 1862 by Don Facundo Bacardi Massó in Santiago de Cuba, Bacardi Limited has grown into the third largest spirit company in the world and the largest privately owned spirit company. Headquarted in Bermuda, Bacardi joined the whisky world in 1998 with its acquisition of the Dewer's brand and five Scotch distilleries: Aberfeldy and Royal Brackla in the Highlands as well as Aultmore, Craigellachie, and MacDuff in Speyside. In 2007 Bacardi began a $250 million dollar investment in their production of Scotch whisky. The money is going towards building new facilities to increase their maturing, blending, bottling and packaging capacity to meet the growth in global demand.

BEAM GLOBAL

Beam Incorporated was spun off of Fortune Brands in 2011 to focus solely on the production and sale of spirits. The company gets its name from Jacob Beam who began selling bourbon by the barrel in 1795. Currently headquartered in Deerfield, Illinois, Beam is the world's fourth largest spirit company and the largest spirit company in the United States. In 2011 their global sales, which included whiskey, cognac, tequila, rum and vodka, totalled $2.8 billion. They currently own and operate the following whiskey distilleries.

Scotland		Canada	Ireland	United States (KY)
Highland	**Islay**	Alberta Distillers	Cooley	Clermont Plant
Ardmore	Laphroaig	Hiram Walker & Sons: produces Canadian Club	Kilbeggan	Booker Noe Plant
				Frankfort Plant
				Maker's Mark

BROWN-FORMAN

Headquartered in Louisville, Kentucky, Brown-Forman was founded in 1870 by George Garvin Brown. As of 2011 they were among the ten largest spirit companies in the world with total net sales of $3.4 billion which included about 90 million liters of Jack Daniel's Black Label Tennessee Whiskey. Besides the famous Lynchburg distillery that produces Jack Daniel's, they own and operate the Brown-Forman, Labrot & Graham, and Early Times distilleries in Kentucky as well as the Canadian Mist distillery in Ontario, Canada.

BURN STEWART DISTILLERS LIMITED

Headquartered in East Kilbride, Scotland, Burn Stewart is a subsidiary of CL Financial, a Trinidadian based industrial conglomerate. They own and operate three Scotch distilleries: Deanston, in the Highlands; Tobermory, on the island of Mull; and the Islay distillery, Bunnahabhain. In 2010 they had

£3.7 million in net sales. While they produce a couple of single malts their flagship product is Scottish Leader Blended Scotch Whisky.

GRUPPO CAMPARI

Originally founded in 1860, in Milan, Italy, Campari has grown to be the sixth largest spirit company in the world, In 2011 their net sales of spirits was €975.1 million. They purchased the Glen Grant distillery of Speyside in 2006 which produces a single malt and the base of their blended Scotch. In 2009 they purchased the Boulevard Distillery which produces Wild Turkey Kentucky Bourbon. They also own and operate the Hueblein do Brasil distillery which produces a number of blended whiskies for the Brazilian market.

DIAGEO

Diageo was formed by the merger of Guinness and Grand Metropolitan in 1997 to form the world's largest producer of spirits. The name comes from the two Latin roots dia for day, and geo for world which refers to their desire that everyday their products would be enjoyed around the world. Headquartered in London, they have a market capitalization of over £35 billion and sold 160 million liters of Johnny Walker in the last six months of 2011. They currently operate the following whisky distilleries:

Scotland				
Highland	Islands	Islay	Lowlands	Speyside
Blair Athol Clynelish Dalwhinnie Glen Ord Oban Royal Lochnagar Teaninich	Talisker	Caol Ila Lagavulin	Cameronbridge Glenkinchie North British Distillery	Auchroisk, Benrinnes Carduh, Cragganmore Dailuaine, Dufftown Glendullan, Glen Elgin Glenlossie, Glen Spey Inchgower, Knockando Linkwood, Mannochmore Mortlach, Roseisle Strathmill

Canada	Ireland	Kenya	United States
Cascade, Gimli	Bushmills	United Distillers and Vintners Ltd	Bulleit (KY)

EDRINGTON GROUP

Headquartered in Glasgow, Scotland the Edrington Group was founded in 1961 through the consolidation of Robertson & Baxter, Highland Distilleries, and Clyde Bonding Company. According to their corporate history, the Robertson sisters consolidated the three companies they inherited from their grandfather William A. Robertson as a means to protect them from a hostile take over. They own three Scottish distilleries: Glenturret in the Highlands, Highland Park on the Isle of Orkney; the Macallan distillery in Speyside, which sold over 6.3 million liters in 2011. They also own a 50% share of the North British Distillery in Edinburgh. Besides single malts they also own Cutty Sark and The Famous Grouse, Scotland's best selling blended whisky.

PERNOD RICARD

Headquarter in Paris, France and founded in 1975 by the merger of the two anis-based spirit makers, Pernod SA and Ricard SA, they immediately entered the whisky market with the acquisition of the Campbell Distillers. Currently they are the world's second largest spirits company with net sales over €7.6 billion. In the 2010-2011 fiscal year they sold 56.7 million liters of Ballantine's Blended Scotch Whisky, their best selling whisky. They currently own and operate the following distilleries:

Canada	Ireland	Scotland	
		Lowlands	Speyside
Hiram Walker & Sons: produces Walker Special Old and Wisers	Midleton: produces Jameson and Tullamore Dew	Strathclyde	Aberlour, Allt-a-Bhainne Braeval, Glenallanchie Glenburgie, Glenlivet Glentauchers, Longmorn Miltonduff, Strathisla Tormore

SAZERAC

Founded in 1869 and currently headquartered in Metairie, Louisiana, Sazerac is a large privately owned company that shares very little information about the size of their company or their brands. They produce a number of premium brands like Blanton's Single Barrel, or Pappy Van Winkle as well as non-premium brands like Ancient Age or Kentucky Gentleman. They currently own and operate the following distilleries:

Canada	Ireland	United States	
		Kentucky	Virginia
Kittling Ridge Winery & Distillery	Penderyn	Buffalo Trace Sazerac Tom Moore Distillery	A. Smith Bowman

WILLIAM GRANT & SONS

Headquartered in Bellshill, Scotland and founded in 1887, William Grant and Sons Ltd is a privately owned spirits company and the third largest producer of Scotch whisky. Because they are privately owned they do not release information on their volume of sales or whisky production. In 2012, William Grant & Sons announced that they would invest €35 million to bring the production of Tullamore Dew Irish Whiskey back to Tullamore, Ireland 60 years after the original distillery closed. They own and operate the following distilleries.

United States	Ireland	Scotland	
		Lowlands	Speyside
Tuthilltown Spirits Distillery (NY)	Tullamore (Under Construction)	Ailsa Bay Girvan	Balvenie Glenfiddich Kininvie

SOURCES

Bacardi Limited. "About Us." Accessed August 3, 2012. www.bacardilimited.com/our-company/about-us.

———. "Fact Sheet." Accessed August 3, 2012. www.bacardilimited.com/ PressRelease/FactSheet.

Beam Incorporated. 2011 Annual Review. Accessed August 3, 2012. investor.beamglobal.com/common/download/download.cfm?companyid=AMDA-DRIR9&fileid=551136&filekey=435240B2-8A5D-48C8-A824-921AB7151E32&filename=Beam2011AR-lo_3-12.pdf

Brown-Forman. 2012 Annual Report. Accessed August 3, 2012. phx.corporate-ir.net/External.File?item=UGFyZW50SUQ9MTQ0NjEzfENoaWxkSUQ9LTF8VHlwZT0z&t=1.

Burn Stewart Distillers Limited. "About Burn Stewart Distillers Ltd." Accessed August 3, 2012. www.burnstewartdistillers.com/pages/about-burn-stewart-distillers-ltd.

Davide Campari-Milano S.p.A. 2011 Annual Report. Accessed August 3, 2012. www.camparigroup.com/media/ANNUAL_REPORT_2011.pdf.

Diageo. Annual Report 2011. Accessed July 24, 2012. www.diageo.com/Lists/Resources/Attachments/1060/Diageo%20Annual%20Report%202011_FINAL_APRIL%202012.pdf.

Edrinton Group. Annual Report 2010. Accessed August 3, 2012. www.edringtongroup.com/company/reports/pdf/2010review.pdf.

Keane, Conor. "New distillery sees Tullamore Dew return to roots after 60-year absence." Irish Examiner, March 28, 2012. Accessed August 3, 2012. www.irishexaminer.com/business/kfididojeykf/rss2/

Pernod Ricard. 2010/2011 Annual Report. Accessed August 3, 2012. www.pernod-ricard.com/medias/Finance/PDF/RapportAnnuel/registration-document-%202010-11.pdf.

Sazerac. "The History of Sazerac." Accessed August 3, 2012. www.sazerac.com/ company.aspx.

———. "Our Bourbon." Accessed August 3, 2012. www.sazerac.com/bourbon.aspx.

Maps Noting Whiskey Distillery Locations

Maps are not designed to be completely accurate.
They are meant to be a visual representation of the location and density
of whiskey distilleries by country and continent.

Africa

Australia & New Zealand

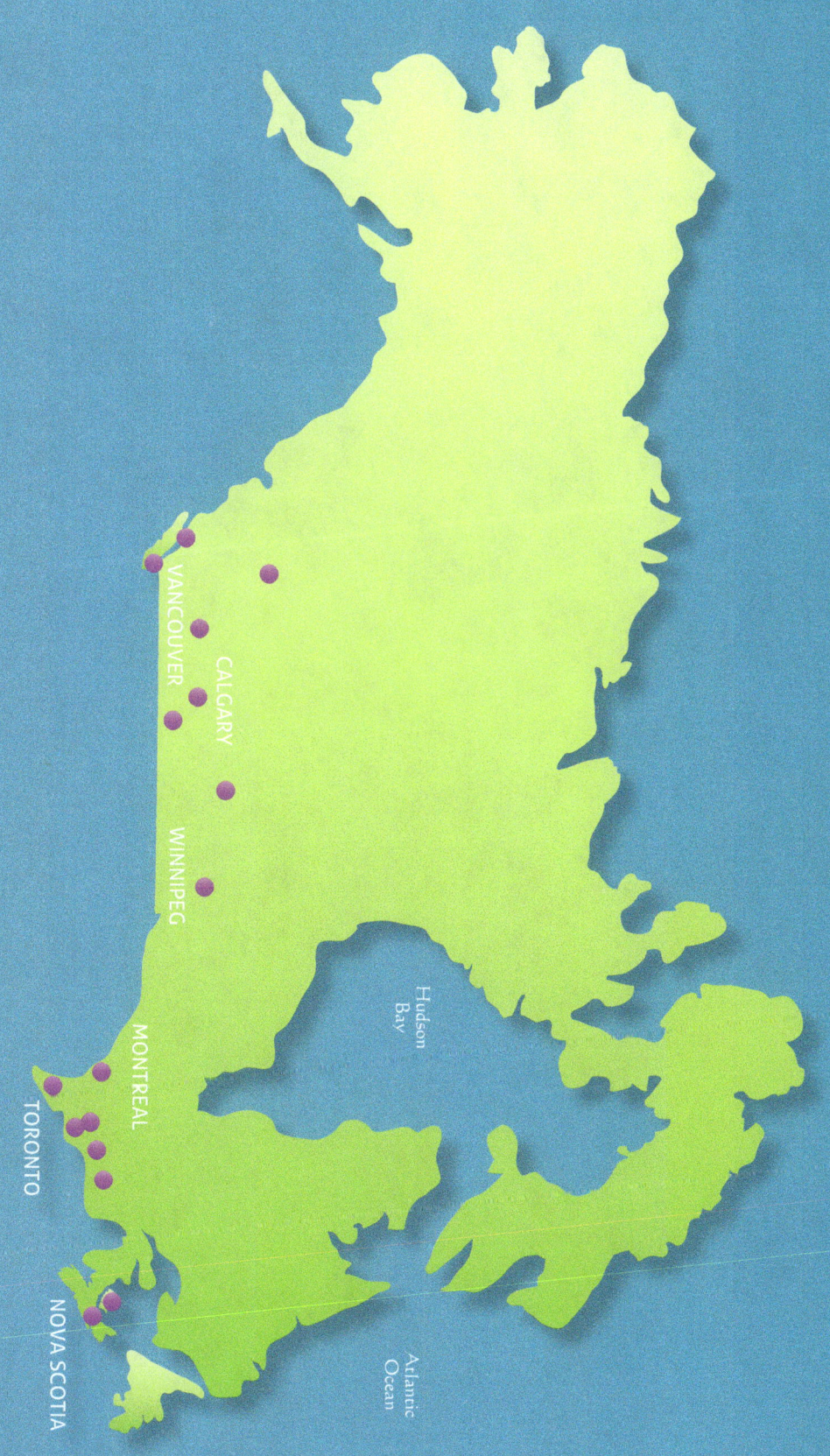

England, Ireland & Wales

Europe

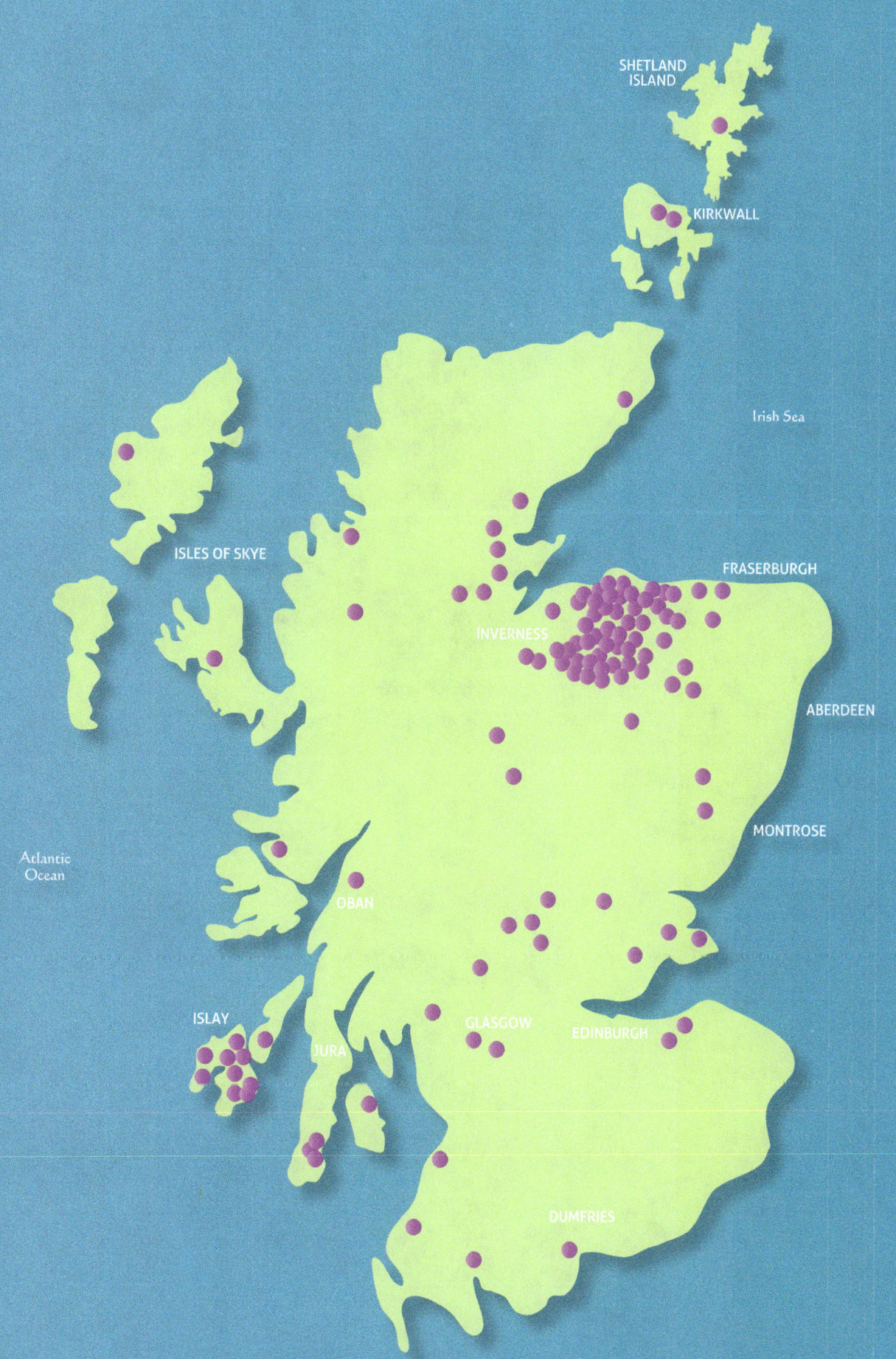

United States Micro Distilleries

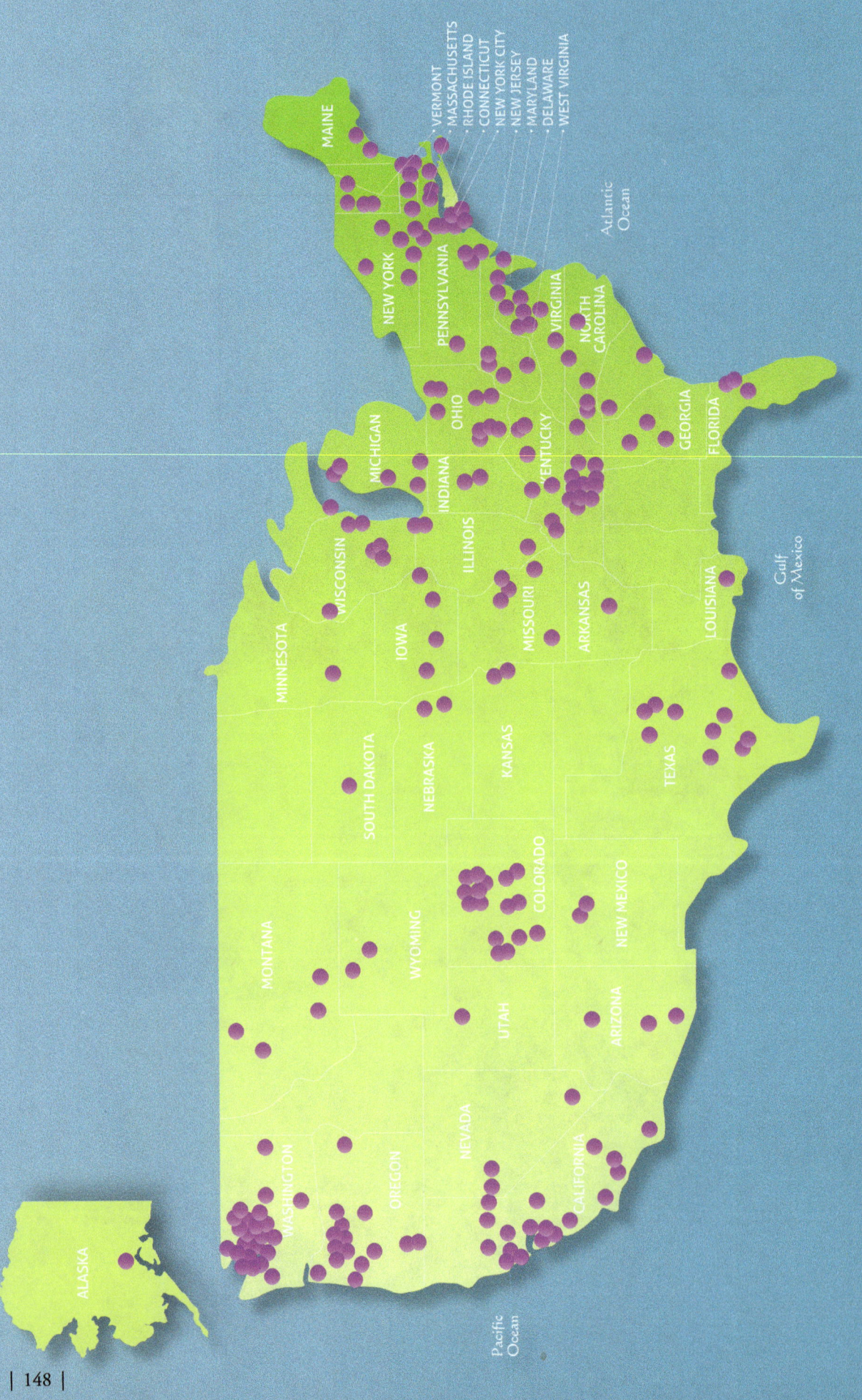

| 148 |

United States Macro Distilleries

| 149 |

Index

A
Angola 5
Australia 21
Austria 27

B
Bacardi 57, 61, 67, 68, 71, 134
Beam Global 51, 57, 65, 76, 85, 134
Belgium 31
Bhutan 9
Brazil 127
Brown-Forman 76, 83, 85, 134
Burn Stewart Distillers Ltd. 59, 63, 65, 134

C
Canada 75
Czech Republic 31

D
Denmark 31
Diageo 51, 59, 60, 61, 63, 65, 66, 67, 68, 69, 70, 71, 76, 79, 85, 135

E
Edrington Group 60, 63, 66, 70, 135

F
Finland 32
France 32

G
Germany 35
Gruppo Campari 69, 83, 127, 135

I
India 9
Inver House Distillers 57, 61, 67, 70, 71
Ireland 51

J
Japan 13

K
Kenya 5

L
Laos 15
Liechtenstein 40

M
Mexico 127
Myanmar 15

N
Nepal 15
Netherlands 41
New Zealand 23
Norway 41

P
Pakistan 17
Pernod Ricard 51, 66, 67, 68, 69, 70, 71, 72, 76, 136
Philippines 17

R
Russia 41

S
Sazerac 53, 76, 83, 85, 136
Scotland 55
  Campbeltown 57
  Highlands 57
  Islands 61
  Islay 63
  Lowlands 65
  Speyside 67
South Africa 5
Spain 41
Sri Lanka 17
Sweden 42
Switzerland 44

T
Taiwan 17
Thailand 17

U
United States
Craft Distilleries
  Alaska 88
  Arizona 88
  Arkansas 88
  California 88
  Colorado 90
  Connecticut 93
  Delaware 93
  Florida 95
  Georgia 95
  Illinois 95
  Indiana 96
  Iowa 96
  Kansas 96
  Kentucky 97
  Louisiana 97
  Maine 97
  Maryland 98
  Massachusetts 98
  Michigan 98
  Minnesota 99
  Missouri 99
  Montana 101
  Nebraska 101
  Nevada 103
  New Jersey 103
  New Mexico 103
  New York 103
  North Carolina 105
  Ohio 105
  Oregon 107
  Pennsylvania 110
  Rhode Island 110
  South Carolina 111
  South Dakota 111
  Tennessee 111
  Texas 113
  Utah 115
  Vermont 116
  Virginia 116
  Washington 117
  West Virginia 119
  Wisconsin 121
  Wyoming 123
United States
Whiskey Distilleries
  Indiana 83
  Kentucky 83
  Tennessee 85
  Virginia 85
Uruguay 127

V
Venezuela 127

W
Wales 53
William Grant & Sons 65, 66, 67, 69, 70, 105, 136

Z
Zimbabwe 5

www.ingramcontent.com/pod-product-compliance
Lightning Source LLC
Chambersburg PA
CBHW080413170426
43194CB00015B/2801